— NO MORE —
SECRETS

Also By Denise Lang (Grant)

The Dark Son (True Crime)
A Call to Justice (True Crime)
Coping With Lyme Disease: A Practical Guide to Dealing with Diagnosis and Treatment
(Editions I, II & III)
How to Stop Your Relatives from Driving You Crazy!
The Phantom Spouse
But Everyone Else Looks So Sure of Themselves!
Footsteps In The Ocean

Contributor to:

Sexual Violence and Abuse: An Encyclopedia of Prevention, Impacts and Recovery
Past and Promises: Notable Women of New Jersey

Also By Irene Colucci-Lebbad

Contributor to:

Sexual Violence and Abuse: An Encyclopedia of Prevention, Impacts and Recovery

— NO MORE —
SECRETS

A Therapist's Guide to Group Work with Adult
Survivors of Sexual Violence

Denise Lang-Grant, LPC
and Irene Colucci-Lebbad, LCSW

BALBOA
PRESS

A DIVISION OF HAY HOUSE

Interior Graphics/Art Credit by James Lebbad

Balboa Press books may be ordered through booksellers or by contacting:

Balboa Press
A Division of Hay House
1663 Liberty Drive
Bloomington, IN 47403
www.balboapress.com
1 (877) 407-4847

ISBN: 978-1-5043-3385-6 (sc)
ISBN: 978-1-5043-3386-3 (e)

Library of Congress Control Number: 2015908727

Print information available on the last page.

Balboa Press rev. date: 06-26-2015

"So many survivors suffer in silence. 'No More Secrets' provides clinicians with the practical and necessary tools to help survivors of sexual violence through their healing process. Clinicians will benefit from the survivor stories that add color and context to each chapter - highlighting the very real, personal, and powerful impact of this work." -*Patricia Teffenhart, MPA, Executive Director, New Jersey Coalition Against Sexual Assault*

"As a longtime professor in an advanced practitioner and Counseling Psychology doctoral program, and a psychologist in private practice, I am very concerned, and consider myself informed, regarding the high incidence of sexual abuse and its crippling life effects on the victims. "No More Secrets'" in-depth and detailed intervention program succinctly covers all of the bases, and will be required reading in the above programs in which I currently administer and teach, beginning in the fall of 2015. This well-organized guide for professionals by Denise Lang-Grant and Irene Colucci-Lebbad should go a long way towards improving the capabilities of the practitioners who, as noted in the text, often avoid addressing this very complex and devastating clinical pathology." *John E. Smith, Ed.D., Academic Director, Seton Hall University, Professional Counseling Program*

For Alan, my husband and partner in everything meaningful, who created the means and space for me to follow a dream, and whose humor and encouragement keeps me sane.

Denise

For my husband Tom, who has always encouraged me in my advocacy for victims, their families, and loved ones impacted by sexual violence. Your support has made my journey meaningful.

Irene

And to all those survivors who are seeking the road to empowerment. They have continued to inspire us both with their courage.

TABLE OF CONTENTS

# INTRODUCTION

Isabel (name changed) walked into our group for adult survivors of sexual violence and sat down. She stared at us with challenging eyes as we maneuvered nine other people through the curriculum you will find in this guide. When it came time, during the various sessions, for group members to contribute their own experiences, she did not say a word. She did not participate, she did not react – a severe monolith with eyes downcast unless they were to stare at us, the facilitators, with that piercing, challenging look.

But she came...every week. She did not miss a session.

We talked about Isabel during our review of the week's session and preparation for another. We had each attempted to draw her out, with little success. Just a shake of her head and the quiet comment, "I'm fine."

Finally, during Week 10 of group, she finally spoke. We were almost in shock, and her fellow group members – who had looked upon her with a little impatience – sat in utter silence.

"I know you have seen me come here and not participate," she said slowly. "But I have listened to all of you. I have learned from all of you. I finally decided it was safe to talk. I have carried shame with me for most of my life. My brother raped me when I was 13 years old. I got pregnant and had a baby. How could I tell my daughter that her father was my brother?"

Isabel spent a few more minutes describing how at age 13, she was the outcast in her family – not her brother, and the challenges she had to meet – living a lie –for the 30 years since that time, including a couple of therapists who wanted to concentrate on her substance abuse and depression, but ignored her disclosure of sexual assault.

"You people here have finally shown me that I was not and am not alone. And for that, I am very, very grateful," she finished. The rest of the group members sat stunned, and then burst into applause. I think we all had tears in our eyes.

People have asked why we put *No More Secrets* together. Isabel – and millions like her – is the reason.

That amazing guru of Group Therapy, Irvin Yalom, cites Universality, Catharsis, and Altruism among his 11 Therapeutic Factors of Group, but for sexual assault survivors, we find that one of the most salient is the Instillation of Hope and the confirmation that they are not going crazy, but have been the victims of a horrendous crime.

The 12-Week Curriculum we have designed is a Cognitive Behavioral Psycho-educational empowerment model, intended to move group members from crisis to stabilization and then to integration. Keeping in mind that both experienced and novice group leaders will hopefully find this guide useful, we have taken care to include evidence-based techniques that have worked for us in the more than fifteen years, collectively, that we have been doing this specific format. For that reason too, we would also make the following recommendations:

- Group should be facilitated by at least one licensed therapist and a co-facilitator who should meet both before and after each session to explore the unit's impact and participants' responses.
- No more than 10-12 should be in the group (we have found that 8-10 is an ideal number), which can be a minimum of 90 minutes to 120 minutes a session.
- Participants in this adult group should be at least 18 years of age, although the 18 to 24 year old range is more appropriate for our college-age curriculum. And while all-females are often the norm, the group can also work with both genders as initial suspicion quickly morphs into understanding that both genders share the same feelings of victimization. (Stay tuned for our Male Survivor's Group and Teen and College Student's Group curriculum guides).
- Prospective group members should be pre-interviewed, as those with pervasive mental health issues and/or severe disabilities need a group tailored to their specific challenges; not this group.
- Group members who miss three sessions will be asked to wait for the next 12-week group cycle, and members should agree that there will be no contact with each other outside of group for the duration of the group. We learned, all too clearly, how disastrous contact can be when unseen issues compromise the safety of the group space.

Finally, we heartily welcome your feedback and stories (contact information provided at the end) as you navigate the sometimes very intense waters of sexual violence and guide others to the shores of healing and recovery. You are choosing to do good work!

Denise Lang-Grant   Irene Colucci-Lebbad

PART I

A THERAPIST'S INTRODUCTION TO SEXUAL ASSAULT

CHAPTER 1

What Do I Say When a Client Discloses?

Sara, 22, was driving to visit her sister in another town. Stopped at a red light, three young men jumped in her car, put a gun to her head, directing her to drive to a deserted road where all three raped her. Injured and in shock, she managed to get herself to a hospital where she received help. Ten years later, however, she is the veteran of numerous failed relationships and has been fired from two jobs. When she sought therapy, the therapist suggested she join Alcoholics Anonymous to deal with her drinking problem. She says she has, before she considers "a more permanent solution" but is still plagued with flashbacks, panic attacks and hyper-vigilance.

Lorna is a petite 57 year old with the slightest trace of a Southern accent. When she talks about how her uncle raped her at the age of five, and continued to do so until she was eight, her eyes still fill with tears. She recalls that when she told her mother about the terror she felt when her uncle was around, her mother slapped her. Married to an abusive man for forty years now, she has been in and out of therapy for years, but her therapists told her the abuse happened so long ago, "it wasn't relevant" to her problems of depression and over-eating.

To anyone who knows him, Geoff appears to be the picture of calm and success. A school principal who is much in demand as a motivational speaker for adolescents, few know that his sexual abuse at the age of 8 by a family friend, and molestation by his priest at 14, has left him with a lifetime of nightmares, suicide attempts, and self-medication with alcohol. Too ashamed of the many doubts regarding his sexuality and depression to disclose his childhood abuses to the medical professionals who treated him over the years, he finally called a suicide hotline in tears. The mental health professional who responded suggested he see a psychiatrist for anxiety medication.

According to the United States Department of Justice:

- One out of four girls and one out of six boys are sexually assaulted by the time they are 18 years old and 30% of child victims are between the ages of 4 and 7;
- One in four college women have been assaulted or suffered an attempted assault;
- 86% of women, 93% of teens, and 97% of people with disabilities who were assaulted knew their attackers;
- One in five children are solicited sexually on the Internet;
- An estimated 39 million survivors of childhood sexual abuse exist in America today;
- Arrests are made in only 37% of cases and only 2.5% of rapists are convicted.

But this problem is not restricted to the United States or even war-torn Third World countries where women and children are routinely raped by invaders. According to the United Nation's Secretary-General's 2006 In-Depth Study on Violence Against Women, it is estimated that one out of five women will become victims of sexual assault during her lifetime – worldwide – including such "civilized" countries as Great Britain, Switzerland, and Australia.

Sexual assault and abuse is a social epidemic, labeled "the" most underreported crime by the United States Department of Justice, and is the deep, dark, dirty secret that is often at the root of substance abuse, depression, and suicide attempts.

It is also such a frightening topic for therapists that often, when a client discloses a sexual assault to his or her counselor, said counselor may unintentionally confound the problem by panicking, minimizing the psychological fallout from the abuse, and choosing to treat the symptoms – the substance abuse, depression, mood swings, hyper-vigilance, trust issues, and relationship problems – rather than the assault itself.

Why? Because even well-meaning and experienced counselors are misinformed and reluctant to delve into an area where they have little or no training. And as human beings, they—like all of us—are also products of their own cultures, religions, families of origin and social upbringing.

First – an important definition: Rape is the social term; sexual assault is the legal term. From the 1920s until 2011, The FBI's Uniform Crime Report (UCR) defined rape as "carnal knowledge of a female forcibly and against her will." This definition covered only penetration of a woman's vagina by a penis, and excluded other forms of sexual violence.

In January 2012, revisions to the UCR's definition was broadened to expand the type of victims and cover multiple forms of sexual violence. The new definition of sexual assault is "penetration, no matter how slight, of the vagina or anus with any body part or object, or oral penetration by a sex organ of another person, without the consent of the victim." (FBI, 2012).

In addition, most states have their own statutes governing the definition of sexual assault that might include the following language: Sexual Assault is any vaginal, oral or anal sex without the victim's consent, *or with a victim who is unable to give consent* (i.e., a victim under the age of 16, mentally impaired, or whose mental faculties is impaired by drugs or alcohol).

Despite a popular culture that flaunts graphic sexual situations (television and the media) and continually minimizes sexual assault through jokes and innuendo ("Get her drunk; maybe you'll get lucky!" – clearly satisfying the definition of sexual assault in that *she* may be incapacitated and unable to give consent), sexual assault is not an easy or polite subject about which to talk when the talk is serious. In fact, it is downright frightening.

As early as the 1970s, Susan Brownmiller was writing about the devastating effects for women of the widespread and 'insidious' fear of rape, and a study conducted in Queensland, Australia in 1992 on 412 subjects concluded that a fear of rape/sexual assault could be termed a "universal condition." So one would naturally think that, like most other fears and emotional conditions, mental health professionals today would be prepared to not only identify the signs of post sexual assault conditions but be able to implement relevant interventions. Unfortunately, this is not so.

In our fifteen years of experience in performing intake evaluations of sexual assault survivors, we have found that approximately 75 percent of those who had previously disclosed to other mental health professionals regarding their victimization, were told a variation of one of the following:

- "That (childhood incest) happened so long ago, I think we should concentrate on your depression and trust issues instead;"
- "I can see where that could have been a problem, but I think the more pressing issue is your drinking and how it is harming your marriage;" (said to a male survivor)
- "That must have been terrible for you, but you were brought here to deal with your substance abuse, we'll talk about your rape *if* we have time."

In each of these cases, the therapist minimized the client's trauma and sexual assault, while focusing on the more obvious mental health condition that is less threatening to address. In doing so, the therapist unwittingly re-victimized the client.

The link between sexual assault and the abuse of substances, and sexual assault and other mental health problems such as depression has been an ongoing source of study over the last twenty years by the World Health Organization and for researchers like Dean Kilpatrick of the National Violence Against Women Prevention Research Center at the Medical University of South Carolina. Among the statistics shared are:

- Almost one-third (31%) of all rape survivors developed Post Traumatic Stress Disorder (PTSD) sometime during their lifetime and more than 11% still fight it;
- Rape survivors were thirteen times more likely than non-victims of crime to have attempted suicide;
- Rape survivors are twenty-six times more likely to have two or more serious drug abuse problems than non-victims;
- Rape survivors are five times more likely to have abused prescription drugs, six times more likely to have used cocaine and ten times more likely to have used "hard drugs" other than cocaine then non-victims.

It becomes obvious that survivors of sexual abuse and assault are likely to use substances in order to numb out from the flashbacks, anxiety, and other symptoms of Rape Trauma Syndrome (See Chapter 3) and this may actually be what gets them through the door of a therapist's office. While most therapy models direct that one addresses the substance abuse first and *then* the co-morbid condition, we suggest a re-thinking of that policy to at least acknowledge the client's underlying cause at the very least, and – in some cases – treat both conditions concurrently.

So What Do I *Actually Say* When a Client Discloses to Me?

We have adopted a Strengths Perspective when someone discloses – whether on a hotline call, in a psychiatric ward, at a substance abuse support group, or in the office. Identified and championed by Dennis Saleebey, the strengths perspective means that everything you do as a therapist will be based on facilitating the discovery and enhancement of the client's strengths and resources in order to help them realize their goals and even dreams.

What this means for the client is a validation of his/her feelings, trauma, and ability to survive one of the worst experiences a human being can experience. Suggested responses could be:

- "Thank you for trusting me with that information. It takes a lot of courage to say those words out loud and that tells me something about your core strength."
- "I am so sorry that happened to you. The fact that you are asking for help tells me just how strong you have been to survive – because only the strong ask for help, not the weak."
- "How terrible for you! Let's talk about how the assault affected your life and how you have managed to survive to this day."

You get the idea. The assault or childhood abuse must be addressed, validated, and the client allowed to feel that they have accomplished something – particularly if and when they reach out for help.

We will address the signs of sexual trauma, but first we want to take a look at some of the cultural myths of sexual assault that prevents most survivors from coming forward…and many therapists from feeling comfortable in responding fully.

CHAPTER 2

Myths of Sexual Assault & Their Effect on All of Us

Imagine leaving a business meeting one evening and walking to your car to go home, laptop slung over your shoulder. Suddenly a mugger approaches from behind, knocks you to the ground, and steals your laptop. Struggling to your feet, you punch in 9-1-1 on your cell.

When the police arrive, you shakily relate what happened. The officer looks you up and down and skeptically begins to question you as to why you are on the street at 10:30 at night (because NO business meeting lasts that long), why you are wearing a good suit (which is just asking for trouble), and why you didn't fight to hang on to the laptop.

Sound far-fetched? Of course. Yet sexual assault survivors often face such questioning and worse in the aftermath of the crime – and not just from un-informed law enforcement. They can face it from members of the helping professions, their family and their friends.

Why? Because there are a number of myths that still permeate our culture regarding sexual violence. Outstanding organizations such as RAINN (Rape, Abuse, Incest National Network) and the NSVRC (National Sexual Violence Resource Center), as well as individual state advocacy groups like the Pennsylvania Coalition Against Rape, and most college campuses address the most common myths that can skew both a survivor's perspective and their subsequent treatment by others.

The U.S. Department of Justice Office on Violence Against Women compiled the following myths of sexual violence that have developed over the generations. We have countered with the facts.

MYTH: *Sexual assault is a crime of passion.*

FACT: Sexual assault is an act of control and aggression. It is less motivated by the desire for sex (except in the thankfully very small percentage of sadistic rapists) and more motivated by the need to exert power and control over another human being. Dr. David Lisak, professor at the University of Massachusetts and leader in studies of what he termed "the undetected rapist" produced research that indicated that approximately 85 percent of sexual assaults are planned – not crimes of passion.

MYTH: *You can easily identify sexual offenders.*

FACT: The stereotypical image of the rapist is that he is "abnormal" and easy to identify. In media, rapists are often of portrayed as deranged criminals and many look that way who you might see on the sex offender registry. But the majority of rapists act and appear relatively "normal" and can hold positions of respect and power. Serial "acquaintance rapists" are often extremely charismatic.

MYTH: *Strangers commit the highest percentage of rapes.*

FACT: While we usually warn our children about "stranger danger," the disturbing fact is that most victims – children, adolescents, and women -- are sexually assaulted by someone they know —someone who has already been identified as safe and non-threatening. In college, acquaintance rape accounts for approximately 90% of completed and attempted sexual assaults. Community surveys reveal that approximately 80% of all rapes, including those against males, are acquaintance rapes. And for those with disabilities, that number skyrockets to as high as 92%.

MYTH: *If you stay out of deserted alleys and other isolated places, you should be safe from sexual violence.*

FACT: Sexual assaults happen anywhere and anytime. Sixty percent of assaults occur in the home of either the victim or the assailant. Sexual assaults also occur in public institutions, the workplace, schools and vehicles as well as places traditionally identified as dangerous— parks, alleys, dark streets, and underground garages.

MYTH: *A victim has to say "No" for it to legally be considered a sexual assault.*

FACT: Any time someone is forced to have sex against their will, it is sexual assault. There are many reasons why a victim might not physically fight their attacker including shock (remember, most victims know and trust their rapist), fear, threats or the size and strength of the attacker. And many sexual assault victims freeze when they are assaulted because the cognitive executive function in their frontal lobe shuts down, rendering them incapable of speech. In addition, there are many other reasons a victim might not say "no" and it is still sexual assault. Dr. Scott Hampton, Director of New Hampshire's Ending the Violence, has spent decades studying and teaching about consent issues and created "25 Reasons Why Sexual Assault Victims Don't Say No." Included among them are: She is too young to know the difference; She comes from a culture where "no" is not an option; She dissociates when she is threatened; She doesn't understand English very well; and She was afraid her boss would fire her.

MYTH: *You can identify rape survivors by their massive physical injuries.*

FACT: The National Violence Against Women Survey found that 69% of the victims were not injured, while 31% did receive some injuries (Tjaden & Theonnes, 1998). Many rape survivors are not visibly injured because the threat of violence alone is often sufficient to cause a victim to submit to the rapist, to protect herself from physical harm. Regarding the survivor's emotional state, both the expressive (cry, laugh, pressured speech) and controlled reactions are normal (see Chapter 3).

MYTH: *Women lie about rape as an act of revenge or guilt.*

FACT: Only about 2% of all rape and related sex charges are determined to be false—the same as other felonies – as supported by FBI statistics. False claims of auto theft are reported more frequently than those of rape.

MYTH: *It is virtually impossible for a male to be raped.*

FACT: Men *are* sexually assaulted. Between one in six and one in ten males are sexually assaulted during their lifetime. A majority of male survivors were assaulted when they were children or teenagers (think about the "hazing" of athletic team members), yet adult men can be assaulted as well. Any man can be sexually assaulted regardless of size, strength, sexual orientation, or appearance.

MYTH: *Gay men represent the greatest danger to boys and other males regarding sexual violence and abuse.*

FACT: Most men who sexually assault other men identify themselves as heterosexual. This fact helps to highlight another myth-buster —that sexual assault is about violence, anger, and control over another person, not lust or sexual attraction.

MYTH: *If a male or female victim's body responds or reaches orgasm during a sexual assault, it means that the victim was enjoying the act and it is, therefore, consensual.*

FACT: Erection and orgasm are physiological responses that may result from mere physical contact or even extreme stress. These responses do not imply that you wanted or enjoyed the assault and do not indicate anything about your sexual orientation. Some rapists are aware how erection and orgasm can confuse a victim of sexual assault. This is why they may manipulate their victims to the point of erection or orgasm to increase their control and to discourage any reporting of the crime.

MYTH: *The number of alleged victims recanting proves that nothing happened and the report of a sexual assault was false.*

FACT: Recanting does not mean nothing happened. Recanting can occur for a variety of reasons such as a victim may worry about how the media scrutiny will impact their lives/families, some feel pressured to recant, and others may face retaliation or fear for their safety particularly in this technological era where anyone can be found and privacy is increasingly non-existent.

CHAPTER 3

The Signs of Sexual Trauma

Back in the late 1960s and early 1970s when American troops were coming back from the war in Vietnam, there began to emerge a cluster of trauma symptoms that – in previous wars might have labeled a veteran as "shell shocked" – but eventually became identified as Post Traumatic Stress Disorder or PTSD.

Two women in Boston who worked in the emergency room of the city hospital in 1974, psychiatrist Ann Wolbert Burgess and sociologist Lynda Lytle Holstrom, began to identify similar symptom clusters in rape victims.

This cluster of symptoms became known as Rape Trauma Syndrome (RTS) and whether you are looking at the DSM IV or 5, they also satisfy the criteria for PTSD. The task for the therapist is to normalize these symptoms for the survivor and help him or her to develop coping mechanisms that will contribute to a healthier, less restricted lifestyle. The interesting thing about the symptoms is that, initially, many of them are the mind's way of protecting the sexual violence victim, giving them time to process what has happened, and begin moving down the path of normalcy. What often happens, however, is that the survivor gets stuck in a few or more of the symptoms and begins to feel as if she or he is "going crazy." This, in turn, can lead to suicidal ideation or even attempts.

The National Women's Study conducted by the National Violence Against Women Research Center at the Medical University of South Carolina found that a full third of all rape victims developed clinical PTSD/RTS, 33 per cent admitted that they had seriously thought about committing suicide, making them 13 times more likely than non-victims to actually attempt suicide.

The signs and symptoms of sexual trauma manifest in three stages, depending largely on the proximity of the sexual assault. Adult survivors, who are seeking help after a history of childhood sexual abuse, may have experienced the acute phase of Rape Trauma Syndrome while they were children, but they can be stuck in the Reorganization or Resolution phases and need help moving on.

The Acute Phase

The Acute Phase of Rape Trauma Syndrome occurs during the sexual assault and immediately afterwards. During the assault, the victim can experience shock, fear, immobility and a primal terror. Particularly when the assault is by a family member, friend or acquaintance, the victim is often in a state of numb denial regarding being assaulted and may freeze. (This often results in the survivor's guilt during the next phase of RTS).

There is increased blood pressure, heart rate and nausea, physical shock and sensitivity to stimuli.

After the assault, the survivor may react in one of two ways:

- Expressed – where he/she is crying, shaking, laughing, shouting, tense and restless, or
- Controlled – where the survivor appears almost unnaturally calm, rational, withdrawn, silent, distracted, disoriented or dissociative.

This second type of reaction can confuse both the medical team and law enforcement, if the survivor is taken to an emergency room – particularly if there are no apparent physical injuries. Comments like the following are often uttered by the survivor:

"It was just a rape. No big deal."
"I must have done something to bring this on."
"He probably didn't mean to hurt me."
"I have to get over this. But all I want to do is sleep."
"Now I'm damaged goods."
"It will go away if I try not to think about it."

This stage can last from days to weeks after the assault, during which the survivor can be emotionally labile. These are all normal reactions and, especially if the trauma reaction is very unlike the survivor's usual personality type, they can harbor guilt and shame for years that impinge on their abilities to lead a healthy life.

Reorganization Phase

This is the phase where the Rape Trauma Syndrome/PTSD becomes most apparent. In Chapter 5, we focus on RTS and PTSD, but the following are most evident and can last for years.

- Numbing
- Guilt
- Fears
- Nightmares
- Suicidal ideation
- Depression
- Trust issues ("I'll never be able to trust anyone again!")
- Anxiety and Panic Attacks ("I think I must be going crazy.")

- Self-blame ("I should have prevented this.")
- Isolation
- Sleep disturbances ("When I sleep, I have nightmares. They won't stop!")
- Eating disruption/Eating disorders ("I can't swallow." "If I eat a lot and get fat, then no one will look at me and I won't be raped again." "I could not control the attack but I can control what I put in my body.")
- Flashbacks – Multiple triggers dealing with the senses – smells, sounds, someone who looks like the offender;
- Disorientation and confusion – Many have difficulty concentrating on anything and can be diagnosed with ADHD.
- Hyper vigilance ("I have to know who is around me at all times, so I don't go to shopping malls anymore, or to movies, or anywhere that there might be strangers.")
- Doubting oneself and one's own judgment about anything ("If I made such a poor decision before that got me raped, how can I trust any decision I make?")
- Anger – Anger at the system (police, courts, attorneys etc.), at the loss of control, at parents/siblings, at others who do not understand or believe, at teachers and peers, at the rapist.

We deal with anger extensively in Chapter 10 because it truly is the backbone of the healing process and an emotion that most try to rationalize. We often tell survivors that "Anger doesn't have a brain; it just is" and following a sexual assault, the survivor often does not know where to put the anger that bubbles to the surface. And all of these symptoms, including anger, can and do impact the survivor's relationships – both close, intimate ones, and even those in a work or school arena.

Again – all of these reactions are normal and the savvy therapist will validate the survivor's feelings and actions as coping mechanisms that developed to deal with an extraordinary event – their sexual assault.

Also during the Reorganization Phase, a number of somatic presentations can become apparent. These range from cardiovascular problems to those involving the gastrointestinal tract, respiratory challenges, neurological issues, gynecological issues, low back pain, and chronic fatigue (often hand in hand with depression) (Kessler, R.C. et al (2000) Journal of Clinical Psychiatry, 61 (5).

The Reorganization Phase is also where the survivor's coping skills – both healthy and unhealthy – become apparent. Addictions (See Chapter 1) of all kinds ranging from drugs and alcohol to obsessive running and working out to other rituals that may border on obsessive compulsive (ie, checking all the locks on the doors and windows at home three times before retiring for the night) become part of the survivor's lifestyle.

This can also include promiscuity as well as the other end of the spectrum, celibacy. We have often been told by a survivor, "I don't know what was wrong with me. I was never the type of girl or woman who slept around but after my assault, I found myself almost making a game out of seeing how many men I could screw. And then I hated myself. Am I going crazy?"

The answer, of course, is no. In fact, since rape – sexual assault – invades the very core of a person's being and renders him/her vulnerable and powerless – the expression of taking back one's power can take many forms, one of them being promiscuity. Again, this is a totally normal reaction.

Resolution Phase

This final stage is where the survivor seeks to integrate the trauma into his/her daily life and move on with a healthy lifestyle. It is most likely that the survivors you will find in your group are stuck somewhere in the Reorganization Phase and looking for help with this final resolution.

Some survivors never reach this stage as there are a number of contributing factors that impact the trauma resolution. These include the survivor's support system, validation of their trauma, their self-esteem, their success in dealing with the criminal justice system, and their belief in some form of spirituality.

While flashbacks, hyper-alertness and a lack of trust can linger or return at various points in the survivor's life, the task – with your help – is to develop a new view of him or herself, resolve any feelings towards the offender (this is where issues of forgiveness versus eternal animosity provide rich discussions and processing opportunities), and develop new goals and hopes for the future.

A Word About Suicidal Ideation

Having a suicidal client is among a therapist's worst nightmares. Yet, with a third or more sexual assault survivors experiencing suicidal thoughts, planning, or attempts, it is likely that you will have in your group some members who have a history of suicidal ideation.

In 2009, the Centers for Disease Control embarked on the most ambitious study to determine the connection between traumatic childhood events and later life mental and physical challenges. More than 26,000 adults were included in the Adverse Childhood Experiences – ACEs – study that did in fact show a higher likelihood of substance abuse, depression, cardiovascular disease, cancer, diabetes and suicide among those whose childhoods included domestic or sexual violence, substance abusing family members or family dysfunction due to divorce, abandonment or mental illness.

In 2011, Dr. Sheela Raja published "Adopting Universal Trauma Precautions: Serving Patients Who Have Survived Sexual Violence." In some ways, this balanced the cautions of the ACE study in that it listed suicide protective factors to include attachment networks (Did the survivor have a support system in place?), social skills, creativity (Did the survivor use art, music or writing to express feelings?), religiosity (Does the survivor believe in God or a higher power? How strong is his/her faith?) cognitive capacity (Are there developmental or intellectual disorders to consider?), and feelings of self-worth.

The survivors who make their way to your group, whether they have had suicidal thoughts or not at some point, are exhibiting great strength of purpose to heal. They are looking for validation of their feelings, a way to increase their self-esteem, and the hope that they can absorb the trauma they suffered, learn positive coping skills, and move on to a happier life.

This curriculum – and you – will start them on their way. We promise that each group member will leave changed for the better.

Let's get started!

PART II

THE 12-WEEK GROUP CURRICULUM FOR ADULT SURVIVORS

CHAPTER 4

Week 1: Breaking the Silence: Our Stories, Who We Are

Ray is a 54 year old educator with a doctorate, wife and four children, and is principal of his town's high school. Fighting depression for most of his life and hospitalized for suicide attempts, he finally called his hospital's crisis line and asked for help. Through his tears, he disclosed his sexual abuse at the ages of 8 and 9 by his little league coach.

Ray had kept this a secret all his life, traumatized by the coach's warnings that no one would believe him anyway. This was the first time he had said the words out loud to anyone, including his wife.

Philosophy and Foundation:

Courage is a kind of salvation. It is just as often the outcome of despair as of hope. On the one hand, we have nothing to lose; on the other, everything to gain.

It takes an immeasurable amount of courage for survivors of sexual violence to decide to share their trauma stories and emotional pain within a group format. Often, it is the first time they have broken the silence to disclose the details of that life-altering event in a safe, supportive setting. Disclosure represents the first step in validation and strengthens the healing process of each member.

Learning Objectives:

- Members will learn the Group Therapy format and what is expected of them for the 12 week cycle
- Member's experiences are validated and individuality celebrated
- Reduction in members' feelings of isolation as bonding with other members begins
- Members are encouraged to identify themselves and who they are apart from the abuse
- Members gain knowledge regarding the myths and facts surrounding sexual violence

Group Content:

Group leaders introduce themselves (if there are co-facilitators and we strongly recommend this) and welcome participants to the Group. A comment should be made that it takes a lot of courage to just show up for a survivor's group, so this says something about the strength of each participant.

Facilitator explains that Week 1 will first orient the members to the group process as well as actually beginning the group content.

Housekeeping Activities:

Facilitators distribute and review the following (These can all be found in Appendix A, Week 1):

- Group Registration Form (If facilitators have not done this during a pre-screening process, it should be done at the start of the Week 1 session)
- The 12- week curriculum (Allow for questions)
- The confidentiality agreement (Ask members to sign and return to facilitator)
- Group rules

The facilitator begins a group attendance sheet where members are asked to sign in each week.

Members will also be given a Group Member Self-Assessment sheet (See Appendix A, Week 1) in order to review and determine their own strengths and weaknesses as part of a group experience.

After reviewing all documents, members will be asked if they have any questions, concerns, comments, or expectations regarding the group experience. Members will process whether they feel controlled or safe by having group "rules" in place.

Evaluation Measure:

Finally, a self-report pre-test will be distributed by the facilitator in order to measure members' current emotional baseline. We highly recommend The Depression, Anxiety, and Stress Inventory (DASS) scale, a measurement tool with a basic 42 item questionnaire, shown to have high internal consistency and to yield meaningful discriminations in a variety of settings. Members are asked to use 4 point severity / frequency scales to rate the extent to which they have experienced each state in the past seven day period. Scores range from a minimum of 0 (no distress) to a maximum distress of 3, with "0" being the least depressed / anxious / stressed choice and "3" being the most depressed / anxious / stressed choice per item.

A post-test is administered in Week 12 to compare members' pre-test emotional baseline scores to those after exposure to the 12 week psycho-educational group process. The DASS measurement tool may also serve to evaluate the facilitator's effectiveness as a change agent. While we could not reproduce the DASS in this guide, you can easily find it on the internet at www.depression-anxiety-stress-test.org or any number of university websites.

Ice Breaker Activity: Upon completion of the DASS inventory, the facilitator asks members to pair up and interview one another utilizing a guided questionnaire, "Who Am I?" (See Appendix B,

Week 1) covering hobbies, talents, and other items that defines the individual. Allow approximately 15 minutes for this activity, after which each member introduces her partner to the group. The person who is introduced has the option of sharing with members why they have made the decision to be in a psycho-educational group.

Important Note: Facilitator should point out that each member represents many interests and fulfills a number of roles in life; that they cannot and should not be defined by their sexual abuse or assault. Each member's individuality is celebrated as people apart from the group.

On The Board: Following the ice breaker activity, Facilitator writes on the board – "What Happens When You Tell" and distributes the "Why Tell?" handout to members. This lists some of the benefits of disclosing one's abuse/assault.

Discussion: Facilitator leads members in discussing the entire subject of disclosing one's sexual assault. Topics covered should include:

- If a member has disclosed to someone in the past, who they disclosed to and whether it resulted in a positive or negative experience;
- Members process what they risked in sharing -- what were their initial fears, and whether there was anyone in their life that they wanted to share their experience with but did not;
- Recognition is given to members for their courage in breaking the silence.
- Validation for members who have never disclosed and confirmation that the group experience creates an emotionally safe environment that can be conducive to disclosure throughout the process.

The activity breaks through the secrecy and frees survivors to tell their truth. As they find their voice in the group, members affirm, honor, and validate the self that was traumatized.

Myths Handout: In the last segment of the session, members will expand their knowledge regarding the myths and facts surrounding sexual assault. A hand out of Myths for members will define typical societal myths associated with sexual assault along with the corresponding facts that dispel the misinformation people are exposed to. Examples of myths for members to process will include women "lying about being raped", "only attractive women get raped", and "sexual assault is impossible without some cooperation from the victim".

Session Wrap-Up: The session ends with the facilitator conducting a deep breathing exercise to relax and ground members, and an empowering affirmation spoken in unison: "I Trust My Inner Being to Lead Me in the Right Path".

Potential Challenges:

Due to the nature of this week's topic, coupled with the fact that this week may represent the first time a group member has "broken the silence" surrounding his/her sexual assault, the various dynamics may result in a member decompensating or finding themselves unable to regulate their emotions.

When members "break the silence" and disclose their traumatic experiences, it could also possibly serve to re-traumatize others in the group. An over-zealous member may also monopolize the group and not give other members a chance to find their voice.

Some members may have had a recent assault and despite being in individual therapy, the memory is still raw. Disclosures from others at this time may trigger a flashback, so group work may be premature.

Given all these circumstances, the facilitator must therefore be ready to acknowledge members' concerns and initiate a crisis intervention if necessary. This is one of the primary reasons why we feel a psycho-educational group such as this for survivors of sexual violence should have co-facilitators; one to present the material and keep the group moving, the other to continually monitor the emotional temperature of the room and be free to deal with anyone who finds him/ herself in crisis.

Important Notes:

Despite accepting group members via an intake interview, the facilitator must also conduct an assessment during this first session in order to ascertain where members are along the healing spectrum of victim>survivor >`thriver. If a member still identifies as a victim (versus a survivor) and finds the opening session too traumatizing, he/she may need to continue to process the sexual assault in individual therapy before they can process in a group. Members ready to do group work must self-identify as a survivor in order to get the most out of the psycho-educational group experience.

Finally, as members share stories and connect to each other in the first session, there may be a tendency for group members to want to fraternize outside of the group. The facilitator must be clear about discouraging outside meetings when discussing the Group Rules at the beginning of the session and reminding group members at the end of the session as well. The responsibility of each member is to deal with their own trauma issues. While they may be enthusiastic about being in an environment with others who "get" what they have gone through, they cannot take on the burden of another's traumas until they have completed the group process and have gained emotional equilibrium and ego strength.

Homework:

Facilitator suggests that each group member purchase a journal over the course of the next week. Given a history of maintaining secrecy surrounding their trauma, group members should take the time to reflect in their journals on the power of finding one's voice as a way to recapture the control they lost as victims and reaffirm their truth as survivors.

CHAPTER 5

Week 2: Dealing With PTSD or Why Am I Not Myself?

Philosophy & Foundation:

After her assault by the brother of a friend, Evelyn could not sleep. Every time she closed her eyes, she experienced a flashback. She found herself becoming angry with everyone around her. She was afraid to go shopping because she was anxious that the offender – or even her friend -- who she no longer spoke to – would be there. She began missing work and spent hours huddled in her bed just crying. "I feel like I'm going crazy," she said.

Evelyn was not going crazy; she was experiencing Rape Trauma Syndrome – a form of Post Traumatic Stress Disorder and the normal aftermath of a sexual assault.

Learning Objectives:

- To identify and normalize the symptoms of PTSD/Rape Trauma Syndrome
- To discuss panic attacks and triggers
- To discuss flashbacks, triggers and methods of coping with them
- To introduce the topic of self-soothing

Group Content:

Unfortunately, we can all identify cataclysmic events of major proportion in our lives: the San Francisco earthquake, the bombing of the World Trade Center on 9/11, Hurricane Katrina, and the Sumatra-Andaman Earthquake which resulted in the deadliest tsunami on record, killing more than a quarter of a million people in 14 countries, to name just a few.

A survivor's sexual assault is much like that tsunami. Their lives will forever be divided between "before the assault" and "after the assault." If the rape is the tsunami in a survivor's life, Post Traumatic Stress Disorder (PTSD) is the aftershock. Nothing is ever quite the same. But that does not mean that a survivor's life cannot be healed and more meaningful.

PTSD is a common and normal reaction to a highly stressful or traumatic event. It was first identified as a cluster of symptoms during the Vietnam War. In 1974, Dr. Ann Wolbert Burgess, a psychiatrist, and Lynda Holstrom, a sociologist, co-founding the first crisis clinic at Boston City Hospital, began to document that rape victims were also exhibiting these same cluster of symptoms and gave it the name Rape Trauma Syndrome.

On The Board: Write "Rape Trauma Syndrome" and distribute the RTS handout (See Appendix B, Week 2). Inform Group Members that while some of these symptoms may seem like negative reactions, many are also the mind's way of protecting trauma survivors and giving them space and time to process what has happened to them.

Discussion: Facilitator should take group members through each of the symptoms of Rape Trauma Syndrome, identifying those which might serve a positive function in the immediate aftermath of an assault, which ones can become a problem if allowed to become part of one's life permanently, and which ones are negative. Stress that all of the reactions are normal for what they have experienced.

On the Board: Write "Four Major Problems:

- Flashbacks/Nightmares
- Avoidance
- Physical Distress
- Feelings/Panic Attacks

Discussion: Take each of the above and ask for input from the Group Members

Flashbacks/Nightmares – What are they? Why is this so disturbing? (Generally it is because the memory of the past trauma is appearing to take place in the present and the survivor feels out of control.) What helps? Suggestions can include:

- Tell yourself that you are experiencing a flashback and the event is over and you survived;
- Breathe – Teach the survivors "square breathing" in order to calm down. This is a technique often used by disaster response specialists in trying to stabilize those who have just experienced trauma. In square breathing, one inhales to the count of two, holds their breath for the count of two, exhales to the count of two, and holds it again for the count of two, visualizing a completed square;
- Ground Yourself by taking the time to observe your surroundings, using your senses: slowly look at the colors around you, listen to the sounds that are happening around you, smell the smells around you, and feel the clothes on your body, the earth beneath your feet.
- Give yourself time to recover by doing something nurturing for yourself, whether that means wrapping a blanket around you, making a cup of tea.

Avoidance – It is normal for trauma survivors to avoid the places, people and things that remind them of the assault. These are called triggers, because they can trigger flashbacks/memories of the sexual abuse.

On the Board: Facilitator writes the single word "Triggers" and asks group members to name people, places, things, smells, and physical actions that trigger memories of the assault. These are listed on the board.

- Discuss avoidance of triggers and ask for input from Group Members as to what lengths they have gone to avoid them;
- Discuss why this might be a healthy reaction at first (the mind's way of giving the survivor time to process the trauma and try to make sense of it) but why it becomes limiting in one's life if allowed to continue indefinitely.

Physical Distress – Trauma overloads one's autonomic nervous system. Arousal levels can remain chronically high which can have a serious impact on the body, as evidenced in the RTS symptoms of hyper-vigilance, anger, mood swings, lack of concentration, irritability, exaggerated startle-response, and sleep disturbances. Ask Group Members what physical problems they have experienced.

Feelings & Panic Attacks – A sexual assault is the most personal and invasive kind of attack and, when the survivor knows the offender, as they do in an overwhelming majority of the cases, layers of very strong feelings can impact the survivor's life. Remind Group Members that they have also been the victims of a crime which also impacts a victim's feelings of safety and security.

- On The Board: Ask Group Members for the types of feelings they have experienced in the aftermath of the assault. Be sure to include: Numbness, Anger, Denial, Shame, Invisibility, Guilt and Self-blame, Hurt and Betrayal, Fear, Confusion, Doubt, Revenge and Hatred.
- Panic Attacks: Discuss Panic Attacks specifically. Ask Group Members what they do when they feel the fear rising; how do they cope?

Soothing Myself Because I Deserve It: The final discussion (you can write it on the board or not) is comprised of ways in which the group members nurture and soothe themselves when the feelings arising out of RTS become strong. (If you have not done so already, you can distribute the handout "How to Help a Survivor"). Then, ask them to name some guilty pleasures and other things they can do to be kind to themselves. This will often end the session with some laughter – which is a good thing after such an intense group!

Session Closer: You can use the Square Breathing exercise we discussed above or one we have included in Appendix B, Week 2 that you can reproduce and distribute.

The Positive Affirmation that everyone should say in unison: "I deserve peace and tranquility, and I am learning to find it."

Potential Challenges:

This particular session is probably the most stress-provoking session in the series. Just identifying and discussing the symptoms of RTS and the emotional fall-out sometimes can trigger a panic attack with some members.

The best way to deal with this is to first prepare members for the fact that this can be a difficult session because you will be discussing very strong feelings and situations; that if someone feels herself or himself being triggered, they can get up, step outside, get a drink of water, and breathe. (This is also where having a co-facilitator is essential!) As you progress through the curriculum for the session, make sure one of the co-facilitators is taking an emotional temperature of the room and group members.

Should a Group Member begin to experience a panic attack or disassociation, then you must be prepared to do some stabilization techniques – such as the grounding techniques listed for Flashbacks – and then empower them to self-soothe upon arriving home.

Homework:

Group members should practice a deep breathing exercise whenever they are triggered by flashbacks or experience increased anxiety and difficulty sleeping. In preparation for this, group leaders should find and distribute a deep breathing exercise that can be used by members to de-stress. Before the session ends, do this breathing exercise with the group members.

CHAPTER 6

Week 3: Understanding It Wasn't Your Fault

Philosophy and Foundation:

Guilt and shame are the dual poisons that can kill the life and soul of a human being. It is rare, in today's society, that a survivor of sexual assault or longtime abuse does *not* express guilt and shame – no matter what the circumstances of the assault. No matter what the age, no matter what the weapon, no matter what events led to the survivor being abused…the survivor – more often than the offender – expresses guilt and shame over their own victimization.

Guilt tends to paralyze victims – keeping them "stuck" in a cycle of self-loathing, especially if their body responded to the coerced sexual experience, or they did not have a chance to say no to the abuser. Survivors therefore may hold themselves responsible as they are convinced they could have done something to stop the assault, even in the face of overwhelming odds.

Shame leaves victims of trauma feeling powerless, devalued, and humiliated, thus intensifying psychological wounds. Shame may also be a reaction to being forced by the abuser to participate in the crime.

The goal of Week 3 of Group is to illuminate all the reasons why society and offenders blame the victim and why the sexual violence that fractured their lives was not their fault.

Learning Objectives:

- To process the emotions of guilt, shame and the fallacy of self-blame
- To explore issues of power and control utilized by the abuser
- To generate a cognitive understanding of why survivors are not to blame, beginning with a profile of the predator as an opportunist finding a vulnerable target
- To explore and share victim-blaming messages from the offender, family, friends, religious institutions and popular culture
- To increase members' ability to identify, communicate, and express "fallout emotions" such as betrayal, lack of trust, and negative self-talk

Group Content:

There are four primary cognitive restructuring exercises in Week 3 that are designed to first examine, and then dispel, cognitive distortions surrounding members' self-imposed feelings of guilt and shame.

On the Board: Facilitator should write on the board – "Why the Assault My Fault."

Facilitator should then encourage group members to quietly list and write down the negative self-talk concerning why they hold themselves responsible for their assault/abuse on the handout distributed (See Appendix B, Week 3). All the reasons members disclose are then shared and processed by the group as the facilitator writes them on a board. Various reasons may include other adults, family, or friends who have convinced the member it was their fault, religious beliefs and influences, anatomical response to the assault, not saying no, conflicting feelings about the abuser, and seeking attention.

In addition, if the abuse occurred in the member's family, self-blame is easier to accept than the reality that those adults did not protect him or her. Each point is then examined for its illogical thinking.

On the Board: The facilitator either erases the board or writes next to the original list: "Why the Assault Was NOT My Fault."

In order to replace shame and guilt with reality, a secondary activity asks each member to write out the reasons why the sexual assault was *not* their fault on the handout.

The intellectual rationalizing will infiltrate and replace the emotional self that creates the distortions. It is an opportunity for members to contradict the first exercise and to replace a false belief with a true one. As in the first exercise, all the reasons why the assault was not their faults are discussed and processed.

The third activity examines and compares members' critical "inner" voice – the one that causes guilt and shame – against a more realistic view of their authentic selves. Members fill out each column in the handout in order to compare the critical inner voice with the reality and recognize the cognitive distortion. They will then have an opportunity to share those comparisons with the group.

The final activity in Week 3 teaches members how to make the connection between the abuse and their emotions. Members are given a handout (See Appendix B, Week 3) that discuss how every emotional reaction has a purpose and a part of healing involves the understanding that emotional symptoms are a normal reaction to a traumatic event.

Facilitator leads the discussion by asking members to discuss the conflicting feelings of trust and betrayal and how these conflicting emotions have impacted their lives since the sexual abuse. Discussion should include the intensity of the sense of betrayal – which depends upon the profile of the offender, ie stranger, acquaintance, friend, co-workers, versus family member – and the degree to which the survivor's ability to trust has been impacted.

Facilitator should validate members' ability to own their feelings by identifying, expressing, and communicating them. Understanding their emotions empower survivors to control their own affect and actions while influencing others in the group.

The session ends with the facilitator conducting a deep breathing exercise (any of the ones previously used or a new one of his/her own selection) to relax and ground members. The empowering affirmation spoken in unison to end Session 3: "My Spirit is My Church and there is No Shame there."

Potential Challenges:

Since cognitive restructuring techniques may be new to some group members, the facilitator must be understanding and patient regarding how members emotionally handle and absorb the topic content. There may be members who exhibit resistance to examining their negative self- talk because the trauma may have occurred early in life and their feelings of guilt, shame and self doubt are cemented as their truth.

Also, the abuse may have been perpetrated by someone they once loved romantically, or a relative, or other person in the member's life that they trusted and respected. Revisiting those emotions in order to dispute them may be painful so resistance/avoidance is a natural reaction. It would be advisable for the facilitator to articulate this at some appropriate point during the session.

Since group exposure to cognitive restructuring activities is the first step for those members still struggling with self-blame, the facilitator must check the group's emotional temperature regarding the processing of the new information. Although it may take time for new skills to be absorbed and utilized, resistant members will now have access to the cognitive tools they need when they are ready to work with them.

Homework:

Group members are directed to reflect, note, and journal long-standing negative thought patterns and emotional distortions that feed their guilt and shame, and continue to reflect on the cognitive re-structuring exercises learned in group.

CHAPTER 7

Week 4: How the Assault Changed Your Life

Philosophy and Foundation:

Margaret was sexually abused by her father from the age of four until she was nearly 16 years old. When she told her mother, at around age 12, her mother moved away and left her and her little brother with their offender father, never to return. Margaret finally sought counseling at age 47 after she had found inappropriate "grooming type" emails from her father to her teenage daughter. She confronted her father, finally reporting him to the police, all members of her family and close friends. She was mourning the life she never had...and was shocked when the therapist asked her what strengths she had developed because of the abuse.

When one looks at the negative effects on your life due to sexual assault and abuse, it is sometimes difficult to imagine that you can concurrently develop a set of strengths that may not have developed otherwise. This is not, under any circumstances, to say that being assaulted is a good thing, but we, as human beings grow stronger through adversity rather than pleasant times. This week, we will guide the group members into identifying how the assault/abuse impacted every aspect of their lives, and then integrate the work of Dennis Saleeby and have them identify the strengths they developed because of it.

Learning Objectives:

- Members will identify how their sexual abuse impacted specific aspects of their life and relationships
- Members will identify and name the strengths they developed due to their abuse
- Members will discuss the concept of Courage and how it applies to their lives
- Members will make a commitment to focus on those strengths that will help them heal and make the changes they desire in their lives

Group Content:

Facilitator should distribute the handout with The Wheel of Life (See Appendix B, Week 4) to all group members. As was illustrated in in Week 2, when a sexual assault occurs, the survivor's life is forever split into "before the assault" and "after the assault." While the emotional impact is such that many survivors fear for their sanity, they cannot begin to heal various aspects of their lives until they can cognitively name the specific changes that the assault brought about. This Wheel of Life exercise is designed to do just that.

Facilitator should direct members to look at the pie pieces in the wheel and take the next 15 minutes to focus on how the assault changed their lives in respect to Physical Environment/Safety, Career/School, Money, Health, Friends & Family, Significant Other/Romance, Personal Growth, Fun & Recreation and Spiritual Life. In each of these "pie pieces" they should each write the relevant impact or change experienced.

Even for those who are survivors of childhood sexual abuse who cannot remember a "before the abuse", they can identify how that abuse experience impacted their lives, for example, "I cannot trust anyone in a position of authority, like a doctor, priest, teacher, etc. or "I cannot have sex without going numb, having flashbacks of the rape."

At the end of the 15 minutes, ask group members to share what they have written, going around the room, category by category.

On the Board – Facilitator should write: "Strengths I Developed Because of My Abuse"

Dennis Saleebey is a social worker who has been dubbed the Father of the Strengths Perspective. The basic philosophy is that every person, family and community have innate strengths that have helped them to survive challenges and to that end, he developed five types of questions to assess those strengths. The challenge for this unit is to have the group members examine their own abilities to identify those strengths they developed upon which they can build.

Facilitator should distribute the handout "Naming My Strengths" (See Appendix B, Week 4) and ask group members to put checkmarks by the strengths they can identify in themselves and then add others on the lines below.

For example, Margaret who was mentioned at the beginning of this unit, not only learned to cook and become independent in organizing her own and her brother's school logistics, and social engagements, but she also developed a heightened sense of empathy for others, due to her mother's abandoning the family in the wake of being confronted with her daughter's sexual abuse. So, too, has each survivor developed strengths in order to cope with their sexual assault and the aftermath.

When members have finished identifying their strengths, facilitator should go around the room, asking members to each share a couple of the strengths they have identified in themselves. Discussion should follow regarding whether this was a surprise to them, and their emotional reaction regarding the realization that they have, in actuality, grown stronger through their trauma.

On the Board: The third and final activity for Session 4 is to initiate a discussion of the concept of Courage. Facilitator should simply write the word "Courage" on the board and then ask group members for definitions. Each definition should be written under the word.

Taking a page (no pun intended) from Ellen Bass and Laura Davis' groundbreaking book, "The Courage to Heal", facilitator should lead discussion on how it takes courage every day to heal from sexual violence. While many think that they can vow to heal in a group or private setting and then everything should fall into place, nothing is further from the truth.

The facilitator needs to encourage members to understand that it takes making the decision to heal each and every day and as we look ahead to the next several group sessions, those decisions to heal will be further validated.

Session 4 closes with a calming breathing exercise and the affirmation: "I survived a sexual assault; I can survive anything!"

Potential Challenges:

There are two possible challenges in this week's session. The first is a group member possibly decompensating when they begin to absorb the enormity of the impact on his/her life due to the sexual assault. The facilitator's job, therefore, is to validate the fact that the survivor has not only taken the first huge step in truly healing – identifying what is wrong – but has actually survived all the turmoil and change that the assault brought about.

The second major challenge that crops up in this session is a survivor's denial of having any strengths. True to form in minimizing their strengths and magnifying their weaknesses (something we will highlight in Week 6), it is not unusual for a group member to say sadly, "I don't have any strengths." It is incumbent on the facilitator to start the identification process by pointing out some obvious strengths, such as "I have empathy for other people in pain" or "I have the courage to disclose my assault and ask for help."

Homework:

Members are asked to look at their Wheel of Life and consider their list of strengths. Then, on the outside of the wheel under each category, list what strength will help them make positive changes in each area of their life.

CHAPTER 8

Week 5: Coping Mechanisms and Survival Skills

Philosophy and Foundation:

Eric (name changed) is a former professional athlete who blew his lucrative career and first marriage due to alcohol and drug addiction. After a suicide attempt, he went into a rehab facility and joined AA, but began the cycle of relapsing and then cleaning himself up. During some point during his second marriage, he lost his job and came close to losing his relationship when his wife issued the ultimatum that he seek help for his childhood sexual abuse by his parish priest. Although he was resistant at first, the counseling and group sessions gradually broke through Eric's long-held defenses and he admitted additional sexual abuse at the hands of a family member. As the months went by, Eric was just as surprised as anyone else that he lost his desire for any type of mind-altering drug and often had no alcohol as well in social situations. "When I faced the true cause of why I was always trying to numb out, I didn't need any of those things anymore," he says.

There is an old expression that John Lennon set to music: "Whatever gets you through the night!" When feeling overwhelmed, we all have strategies (both positive and negative) for getting by, compensating for hurts, and dealing with physical and emotional pain. How a survivor of sexual violence interprets and internalizes the experience leads to different psychological responses manifesting in different coping behaviors.

Trauma survivors may self- medicate, minimize negative experiences, engage in risky behaviors, or try to maintain control over every aspect of their lives because the abuse disempowered them. They are looking to self-regulate their emotional states by soothing themselves with maladaptive behaviors, often leading to self-destructive consequences.

Survivors usually don't think about these coping mechanisms consciously, but come back to them again and again because there's an inherent logic there. Underlying each one is a need. If survivors discard a coping mechanism without finding another way to understand and meet that need, the change does not last.

Coping skills ultimately represent survival tools that are needed to provide essential boundaries allowing those traumatized by sexual violence to function in the world.

Learning Objectives:

- Group members identify both negative and positive coping mechanisms that have served them in the past
- Members recognize self-destructive behaviors that are no longer useful or healthy
- Members process how to incorporate positive survival skills into their behavior as healthier ways of coping
- Members are acknowledged for their resourcefulness in staying alive and utilizing whatever they could to survive the trauma
- Members learn to forgive themselves for unhealthy past behaviors and recognize their successes in order to reinforce their own empowerment

Group Content:

Activities in Week 5 revolve around first assisting group members in identifying the coping mechanisms they have utilized (especially those that provoke feelings of shame) and then examining the reasons they used them.

Facilitator distributes List of Coping Mechanisms (See Appendix B, Week 5) .The facilitator will ask members to circle those coping skills with which they identify and then add any others they have used in the lines below.

On the Board: Facilitator draws a line down the center of the board and writes "Negative Coping Sills" on one side and "Positive Coping Skills" on the other. Then facilitator and asks for the members to begin listing those skills that they identified, determining which might be negative or positive. This often requires some processing in that some perceived as positive immediately after the assault (ie. Isolating behavior so survivor can feel safe) may, with time, turn into a negative (ie. The survivor shuns all family, friends, social engagements, school and work).

The facilitator should stress how members' negative coping skills have arisen from an inherent resourcefulness and resilience needed in order to survive.

Discussion: Facilitator should lead an interactive discussion so members will understand how negative coping mechanisms have a logic to them and fulfilled a need at the time. They provided a means for group members get through each day. If no defenses were in place, survivors would have been overwhelmed and unable to manage their lives. Now, since those negative tools no longer serve their purpose, a positive change is needed.

Discussion should then segue to various positive change strategies and examined for integration into members' lives.

Facilitator distributes the handout on "Ways To Nurture Yourself" (see Appendix B, Week 5). Facilitator should ask members if they can think of any other ways in which they can be kind to themselves and these are added to the list. Members are reminded to approach the changes slowly, with love and respect for themselves and their needs, so the changes will last.

On the Board: Facilitator clears the board and writes "Reasons to Forgive Myself."

Discussion: The subject of forgiveness should be addressed in relation to the survivors themselves. Facilitator encourages members to begin to forgive themselves for utilizing a particular self-destructive behavior. Group members are asked to list and then discuss how feeling ashamed can keep members trapped and powerless, too paralyzed to make the positive change. Members should identify and list reasons to forgive themselves for some unhealthy choices, while acknowledging their own resourcefulness in the face of overwhelming emotional distress.

Finally, Facilitator distributes the handout entitled "My Accomplishments" (See Appendix B, Week 5). This handout is primarily blank but important to note that the one accomplishment listed is "I survived a sexual assault/abuse." Since survivors often tend to minimize their accomplishments, members are asked to make a list of the things they have accomplished in their lives so far, giving themselves the credit they deserve for surviving a horrific life event, no matter what type of coping skills they utilized along the way.

Session Wrap-Up: The Facilitator conducts a deep breathing exercise to relax and ground members. The empowering affirmation spoken in unison to end the session: "I am becoming a healthier and happier person each day."

Potential Challenges:

Resistance to changing coping mechanisms expressed by some of the members is the primary challenge in this week's unit, which may or may not actually be articulated during the group session.

Since multiple micro level factors (internalized feelings) and macro level factors (societal and cultural influences) influence and impact a survivor's coping strategy, some survivors will cope with trauma in adaptive ways, while others will not. Some group members may be reluctant to give up their pattern of maladaptive coping skills because it has worked to alleviate their emotional distress and maintained a sort of equilibrium, thus becoming the "norm" by which they are able to function.

The primal reaction here, of course, is fear. Their individual identities may be wrapped up in the negative behavior that evolved into addictive patterns. If a group member has not reached out for help with those issues, they might still be struggling with both the sexual trauma and issues caused by the addiction. Also, some self-loathing may exist on a micro level caused by the maladaptive behaviors that the member has managed to suppress in favor of continuing to maintain the "norm". It is a viscous cycle.

The facilitator needs to point this out, validating the members and reminding them that positive results develop slowly and with patience. This is where a supportive network can be a major assistance. They have the group as one supportive network, and we will be discussing support systems in one of the upcoming group sessions.

Homework:

In order to reinforce the message in Week 5, the Facilitator should ask group members to create a collage (size is of their choosing) illustrating images of positive coping skills and self-care ideas. The images can be taken from magazines, internet, and other print media pages. The collages will be put on display at the start of the following week's session..

CHAPTER 9

Week 6: Recognizing the 9 Trolls of Limited Thinking

Philosophy and Foundation:

Imagine yourself standing on one side of a bridge... traumatized, alone and burdened by the memory of sexual violence. As you look across the bridge, you can see the Golden Light of Healing. It is not that far away...almost within reach! All you have to do is cross that bridge. But as you start your journey to the Healing Light on the other side, you are stopped by Trolls living under the bridge, grabbing at your ankles and preventing you from moving forward! The Troll's names are not catchy, but their grip is powerful enough to stop you from getting to the healing side: Filtering, Polarized Thinking (or Perfectionism), Over-generalization, Catastrophizing, Mind-Reading, Magnifying, the Shoulds, and Emotional Reasoning!

For the first five weeks, we have processed what it was like to disclose one's assault, Rape Trauma Syndrome/PTSD, how the assault changed your life, and negative and positive coping skills. As we finish the first half of the Group Agenda, Week 6 will focus on the negative schemas or limited patterns of thinking – The Trolls – that have been formed as a result of the assault.

Aaron Beck, often called the Father of Cognitive Therapy, originally identified 15 common but harmful and limited thinking patterns – or cognitive distortions – that we all exhibit at times, that restrict our ability to engage in a positive way or attain the kind of happiness to which most people aspire. Particularly for survivors of sexual assault/abuse, however, it is very easy to get bogged down in several of these – and remain in the control of the Trolls – since trauma, itself, froze the survivor's thought processes. As time passes, the negative reaction to any given situation becomes *an automatic thought response*. The only way to break the hold of these harmful automatic responses is to identify, challenge them, and practice the positive alternative.

Learning Objectives:

- Members will identify the 9 Trolls of Limited Thinking and how to challenge them
- Members will explore the idea of automatic thoughts and the rational and irrational processes associated with the negative thought patterns
- Members will identify which limiting Trolls have impacted their ability to heal
- Members will learn to make the connection between their patterns of limited thinking and their levels of emotional disturbance

Group Content:

Facilitator should distribute the handout entitled "The 9 Trolls of Limited Thinking" (See Appendix B, Week 6). You will note that there are no definitions written on this handout. Group members, at this point, should be comfortable enough to take notes for themselves, particularly when they identify with the following descriptions of the Trolls.

As the facilitator explains each Troll, the question should be asked: "Can anyone give me an example when you might have experienced this in your life?" Facilitator should then encourage group members to note their own examples on their sheet, whether they choose to share it with the group or not.

The 9 Trolls of Limited Thinking

- Filtering – This is a kind of tunnel vision that looks at only the most negative element of any situation to the exclusion of everything else, and dwells upon that. A negative detail is picked out and the entire experience is colored by it. Example: You did a good job on a particular project and you're praised for it; your boss suggests that on the next project, you include an additional element. Result – you go home feeling depressed because you think your boss has criticized you for not being thorough. Your fear and sense of loss become exaggerated. A filtering pattern "awfulizes" your thoughts by pulling negatives out of context and magnifying them while ignoring any good comments/experiences.

- Polarized Thinking/Perfectionism – Things are black and white, good or bad, no shades of grey; no room for mistakes. You are either brilliant or an idiot. Emotions are also polarized. Since cognitive interpretations are extreme, emotions become extreme. If you cannot be the best/top of the heap in a class, activity, or social group – you do not participate. When tackling a task, everything must be exactly right, or it is tossed aside. Example: Everyone laughed at the television show Monk, but his contortions over placing a stamp at exactly the same distance from the top and side of an envelope or he threw it out, is an example of polarized thinking.

- Overgeneralization – You reach a general conclusion based on a single incident or piece of evidence and then leave no room for a change of thought. The most commonly heard phrases include : "You always...", "You never...," "Everybody always...," etc. These labels are a knee-jerk reaction (a common description for automatic thought). For example, you ask a friend out to lunch and she says she cannot go. This rejection leads you to think "Nobody ever wants to have lunch with me!" The single biggest emotion here is fear. These global labels may have a grain of truth – but you generalize this grain into a global judgment, despite any evidence to the contrary. Stereotypes are the result of overgeneralization; have a bad experience with a member of a particular culture, and suddenly all members of that culture are jerks.

- Catastrophizing – Catastrophes are everywhere! A small leak in the boat means it will sink and you will drown. A headache means brain cancer. A rejection after a job interview means you will never work again and will starve to death. Catastrophic thoughts often start with the phrase, "What if...?" Survivors of sexual violence are particularly vulnerable to catastrophizing. "What if I go shopping alone and get assaulted again?" "What if I go on a date and he rapes me?" "What if I take a yoga class and the instructor rapes me in the parking lot?" (For someone sexually abused by a teacher, this one combines overgeneralization and catastrophizing!) The result is that the survivor's world shrinks to only the very small expanse he or she thinks they can control – and it keeps them bound up in fear.

- Mind-reading – There are two forms of mind-reading that serve as limited thinking Trolls. In the first, you make snap judgments about people; without their saying so, you believe you know what they are thinking – and react to that. At work here is projection; that is, you are projecting your thoughts and reactions onto someone else. For example, your significant other walks through the door with a frown on his/her face. You immediately jump to the conclusion that they are mad at you; that you did something wrong or they are going to hit you with bad news. Instead of asking, you react with an amped up and defensive attitude.

  The other type of mind-reading is where you expect others around you to know what *you* are thinking. An example is the survivor who is watching an action movie with a significant other, where one of the main female characters is being manhandled roughly. This may trigger a fear response in the survivor, or even a flashback, while the partner is undisturbed. The survivor gets furious with the partner for not responding with compassion or even caring and responds in a snippy way when the spouse asks what is wrong. "If you can't figure it out for yourself, I'm not going to tell you!"

- Magnifying and his Troll brother Minimizing – This is where you exaggerate the degree or intensity of the problem. You turn up the volume on anything bad, making it overwhelming. Small mistakes become tragic failures. Words like *huge, impossible* and *overwhelming* are all possible magnifying terms.

  Now imagine taking a pair of binoculars and turning them around, making all those things that are close up look far away. That is what minimizing does to one's life and self-esteem. "Oh, that's nothing," said while blood is dripping down someone's arm is minimizing. Sexual assault survivors tend to use minimizing to either survive difficult circumstances or when viewing their own assets as insignificant. When a survivor continually magnifies or minimizes, it keeps him/her stuck in an irrational place and unable to move on to healing.

- Personalizing – Like mind-reading, there are two kinds of personalizing to which survivors fall prey. The first involves comparing yourself to everyone else, and coming up short every time. Are you smarter, better looking, faster, wealthier? Even when the comparison might be favorable, the survivor's worth is in question.

The second type of personalizing is when one assumes that everything that people are saying or doing in every situation revolves around the survivor. Example, "My proposal

This type of Troll really grabs hold of survivors. Since a sexual assault is so all-consuming in its impact on the survivor's life, everything done and said by others is minutely examined and evaluated as to its effect.

- **The Shoulds** – In this type of thinking pattern, you are operating from a list of inflexible imaginary and ironclad rules about how you and others should act. The great psychologist Albert Ellis called this "Musterbation" while psychiatrist Karen Horney called it the "tyranny of the should." For Example: "I should (must) always be generous…patient…kind… appear interested…be the perfect daughter/friend/partner/parent…I should never… make mistakes, get tired or be sick."

Survivors of sexual assault often implement these rigid rules for themselves and others as a way of attempting to take control back of their environment, and to feel safe. Unfortunately, often the opposite is the actual outcome.

- Finally, there is **Emotional Reasoning** – Typical of this type of Troll is the automatic thought, "I feel foolish doing this, therefore I am a fool and everyone thinks of me as a fool." This is where the survivor equates an emotion with who they are as a person and, again, usually come up short. "I am envious that my sister has never gone through an assault and has a happy life, therefore I am a bad person."

On the Board: Facilitator writes -- How to Challenge the Trolls!

There are three questions a survivor should ask when involved in a situation where they become aware of rising fear, stress or anger. Facilitator should write these on the board and ask for input from the members:

1. What Troll is at work here and causing an automatic negative thought?
2. What is/could be the reality of the situation in front of me versus what I am reacting to in my head?
3. What am I gaining by hugging the Troll (remaining in the fixed negative thought pattern) as opposed to moving across the bridge?

Session Wrap-Up: Positive affirmation to be said in unison: "I am crossing the bridge to healing!"

Potential Challenges:

The major challenge for this week's session is that there is a lot of material to cover and the facilitator will need to be mindful of the clock. It is the type of session that group members seem to enjoy and most like to share their own situations that illustrate the Trolls. It is then incumbent on the facilitator to keep the group moving.

It is important to note that the facilitator should introduce the Trolls by emphasizing that we all do these things at some point and to some degree, in order to normalize the group members' reactions. Sexual assault survivors, however, are particularly vulnerable to the Trolls as they are struggling to not only renegotiate the work around them and feel safe, but also often have to combat negative perceptions and legal situations of those who are victims of a crime.

Homework:

Group members are encouraged to note in their Journals what Trolls they notice during their week, their responses, and the situation outcome.

 CHAPTER 10

Week 7: Anger – The Backbone of Healing

Philosophy and Foundation:

Feelings buried alive never die.

Of all the different emotions that give rise to anxiety, anger is the most common and pervasive one. It can cripple one's life and result in relationships being destroyed, eating and sleeping disorders, and pervasive depression if the angry feelings are not dealt with. Besides being angry at the abuser, survivors can be angry at themselves for not being able to defend themselves more successfully, at family members for not protecting or validating them, at people who do not understand or know how to help, or the criminal justice system for failing to find or punish the offender.

However, anger expressed in a healthy way can motivate change, be a source of dialogue, understanding, and healing. It is a natural part of one's self-preservation response. When used effectively, anger can strengthen our sense of ourselves as well as improve our relationships.

For sexual trauma survivors, the most logical and appropriate response to abuse is anger. When used as a positive force, it is the backbone of healing and the most effective antidote to hopelessness and depression.

Learning Objectives:

- Group members will identify at whom their anger is directed
- Members will process how anger has impacted their lives and often masked an inner depression, frustration, and shame
- Members will learn how anger may manifest differently in male and female survivors
- Group members will process their individual fears of expressing anger based on their families of origin, cultures or societal rules of behavior
- Members will identify healthier ways in which anger can be channeled so that it can motivate and inspire lasting life changes

Group Content:

On the Board: The Facilitator should draw two large faces, the first one with an angry mouth and labeled "Anger" on the inside of the face and "Depression" on the outside. The other face should have a sad mouth with "Depression" on the inside of the face, and "Anger" on the outside. The facilitator should point out that Anger and Depression are two sides of the same coin. Those who are showing their depression to the outside world are really angry on the inside; and those who are angry at the world are suffering great pain on the inside.

Facilitator should ask the group whether they can identify with either of these faces, or whether they know anyone who fits these categories. Members can process this and whether they have observed that these reactions are gender related.

In our experience, most often, men present with anger while women most often present with depression. This is not to say that exceptions do not exist, but it will allow group members to begin to identify and normalize these two emotions following an assault.

On the Board: Facilitator should write, "How I Learned Anger". The second activity involves members sharing how anger was expressed and dealt with in their families of origin and how those messages impacted their ability to express their own anger in healthy or unhealthy ways. Facilitator will write members' answers on the board.

Facilitator should then distribute the handout labeled: "Anger: Costs/Benefits" (See Appendix, Week 7). The handout is divided into two columns, one labeled "Costs" and the other labeled "Benefits". The Facilitator should then direct group members to list the costs associated with their anger, and then the benefits. Costs can include things like "divorce" or "estranged friendships" and Benefits can include such things as "Activism." The facilitator will write the answers on the board in two columns and the group will process their responses.

In the third activity, Facilitator will distribute the handout entitled: "Dealing Successfully with Anger" (See Appendix B, Week 7). Listed on this handout are some guidelines for dealing with anger and the facilitator should discuss and process each individual guideline with the group.

The guidelines include how to communicate angry feelings assertively, not aggressively ("I" statements vs. "You" statements), and understanding that anger is a choice we make – other people don't make us angry, we choose to get angry (remember the Trolls from Week 6). Facilitators should also provoke a discussion around how to overcome fears about alienating others if the survivor should allow anger to show; letting go of the standard of always having to be nice or pleasing in all situations.

On the Board: Lastly, the facilitator will write "Positive Outlets for Anger" and ask members to explore alternative methods they can utilize to discharge their anger in ways that are not emotionally destructive (ie: effigies, exercising, angry letters confronting the offender or unsympathetic family members that are burned, satisfying rituals, etc.). The facilitator will list and process members' responses on the board.

Session Wrap-Up: The session will end with the facilitator conducting a deep breathing exercise to relax and ground group members. The empowering affirmation spoken in unison to end the session: "I accept all my feelings and will express them in a healthy way."

Potential Challenges:

Of all the emotions, anger seems to be the universally feared one, depending upon what a person learns in their families of origin. If group members received negative messages from their families regarding expressions of anger, or family members were emotionally shut down and did not express anger at all, members will have a more difficult time understanding and processing an emotion with which they may not be comfortable.

Since expressing anger in an appropriate and healthy way involves finding one's voice and feeling empowered, those group members who have suppressed their emotional responses over the years will not only have difficulty with the process of moving away from their "norm", but will also be wary of the change needed to become more assertive. In those cases, the facilitator must be aware of an over-arching clinical depression that many manifest when anger is suppressed and denied for so long.

As an agent of change, the facilitator must utilize positive reinforcement skills, and encourage the healthy expression of anger with members who manifest this emotional impairment, since often those survivors will continue to deny they are angry at all! The point that must be made is that anger is good, healthy, a normal response to being assaulted and learning to identify, accept, and discharge that feeling is a major step towards health and healing!

Homework:

For Week 7, group members will be asked to write a letter to the abuser, parent or other caregiver who did not protect them (whether living or dead). All feelings of rage, anger, and sadness should be written out. Proper grammar is not necessary and writing style can be free association.

The exercise allows members to release feelings that may have been suppressed for a long time. The letters can be brought to group, read out loud if the member wants to do so, and then burned in a group ritual outdoors. The metaphor of burning can bring some closure for those who have never expressed or acknowledged their anger and sadness.

CHAPTER 11

Week 8: Developing Your Support System

Philosophy and Foundation:

Mandy was sexually abused for years by both her father and her grandfather. Kerry was raped by a police officer who stopped her on a deserted road late one night as she was driving home from a friend's party. And Kevin was assaulted by his baseball coach. All three, now well into adulthood, have had problems trusting anyone in their lives – from authority figures to potential romantic partners.

Sexual trauma disrupts the fulfillment of many human needs: trust, safety, self-esteem, power, intimacy and independence. An integral part of healing includes gaining control over one's own life again. Independence – not isolation – is the pathway.

So how does one get it back? The mechanism for healing is a strong support system. However, we must also be able to discern the difference between a healthy support system and an unhealthy, dysfunctional one. In a healthy or "open" system, one can feel valued, heard, and respected. In a "closed" system, dysfunction creates isolation, distrust, lack of support, poor boundaries, disrespect and secrecy. While a knee-jerk reaction might be to look to family as the support system, it is not always the healthiest network.

For sexual trauma survivors, issues of trust often hijack the brain into thinking that he/she is alone and cannot rely on anyone. Especially when the abuse came from within the family, the need to establish personal boundaries and build stronger, more responsive support networks elsewhere represents a key component in the ability to heal.

Learning Objectives:

- Members will define what a true support system means for them
- Members will assess the people in their lives and evaluate them in terms of support
- Members will be introduced to the concept of boundaries as it relates to creating and maintaining a strong support system
- Members will be introduced to the Window of Trust as it relates to setting boundaries
- Members will address creating a safety plan for both family and social situations

Group Content:

The first step in creating a support system is to assess the relationships in one's life today but before we can even create that network, we need to define what the term "support system" means to you.

On the Board: The facilitator writes – "A Healthy Support System" and asks group members to identify the characteristics of a strong and healthy support system. These are written on the board and processed once everyone is finished contributing.

The facilitator then distributes the handout labeled "My Support System" (See Appendix B, Week 8). This handout asks the group member to think about all the people that they normally have contact with on a daily or weekly basis. With the survivor at the center of the "Circle of Trust", the member is asked to write the names of (a) those people in their life that they can totally trust and depend upon in the first ring; (b) the people they can trust and rely on most of, but not all the time, in the second ring and then everyone else in the third ring.

Facilitator should point out that the people in the first ring, and perhaps some in the second would constitute the survivor's support system.

Discussion: Facilitator should lead group members in processing their Circles of Trust. Any surprises? How are they feeling about their support systems that are in front of them?

The third activity involves a discussion of boundaries. Sexual assault survivors have had their most personal boundaries --- their bodies – breached and violated, perhaps multiple times. If they were abused as children, they likely grew up with a fractured sense of what a boundary might be and that they have the right to set them. For that reason, we like to use a modified version of the remarkable Johari Window, created by the psychologists Joseph Luft and Harry Ingham in 1955, to illustrate boundaries (See Appendix B, Week 8).

Facilitator should distribute the Johari Window diagram and explain the four panes, paying particular attention to Windows 1 and 2 (Normally labeled 1 & 3 in the traditional model), emphasizing that it is up to the survivor how far they choose to open the window, based on feedback from the person to whom they are speaking.

On the Board: Facilitator should write "Boundaries I Will Set."

Discussion: The final discussion should center on the issue of boundaries and when they are tested the most, ie. at a family gathering, at work, at school, or during the holidays. Facilitator should solicit from the group members, various boundaries that will make them feel safe (thus constituting a personal safety plan) in anxiety provoking situations. For example: "I will not talk about my assault at a family gathering because they have never been supportive."

Session Wrap-Up: Facilitator can lead group in deep breathing exercise to de-stress and ground them. Positive Affirmation to be said in unison: "I am the architect of my own future! I am in charge of me!"

Potential Challenges:

This week's session, like the remaining four, is designed to empower the group members. The main challenge in this session is the possibility of a group member flatly stating that they do not have a support system or anyone they trust.

The most obvious answer is that this Group and the facilitators are a type of support because the survivor is attending and participating, but – per the rules of Group – this will not be a satisfactory support outside of the weekly group session. And Group will eventually terminate.

This is where the Facilitators need to be creative and can open it up for group discussion as well. Considering the nature of the concerned member's sexual abuse, who might be in that person's life that could lend support…if they were given a chance? This may require a leap of faith on the part of the survivor, but also where the Johari Window exercise also comes in handy.

Homework:

Members are asked to consider their Support Systems/Circle of Trust as they go through their week, being aware of how each regularly held contact fits into their lives and how much they are willing to disclose. They can add or change names on their diagram as the week – and life – progresses.

CHAPTER 12

Week 9: Healing Sexually

Philosophy and Foundation:

Marilyn was sexually assaulted three different times in two different states—the last time, by a construction worker as she arrived at work early one morning to work on her company's books. She has not been able to have sex with her husband since the last assault – six years ago.

Andrew was molested at age nine by a young man his minister father took in off the streets to try and help. He has been married for 15 years and has two children but says he cannot stop feeling that sex is "dirty."

Laura was sexually abused by her father and ignored by her alcoholic mother from age 8 until she was 16. She also is married, with one child, but says she would be happier "living without sex."

Human sexuality is our birthright and a part of our ability to express ourselves as sensual beings. At its best, sexual expression can be uplifting, satisfying, and joyous; reaffirming our humanity and individual natures. At its worst, sex can become a weapon, a means of exercising power and control over another, and a degrading, disempowering experience.

Due to their abuse, the mind set of survivors may rest in the fact that sexual relationships are inherently imbalanced, with one partner dominating and the other submitting. For those victimized in childhood, the initial experience with sex coming from a sexual assault can result in a very confusing idea of human sexuality for the adult. Body memories may trigger them, along with fear, vulnerability, and disgust that can interfere and disrupt normal sexual relations.

Other survivors may become hyper-sexual or promiscuous in a maladaptive attempt to regain control of their own sexuality.

Ultimately, for survivors of sexual violence, there is more despair about healing sexually than about any other aspect of the healing process. It is the part of their lives in which the past most clearly and directly impacts the present. Since survivors have been robbed of the opportunity to develop their sexuality at their own pace, to change sexually requires a kind of consistency and dedication that allows attitudes of self-love and self-acceptance to create sexual empowerment.

Learning Objectives:

- Members will define "Sex"
- Members will gain an understanding of healthy sexuality and consent
- Members will learn to establish healthy sexual ground rules
- Members will compare healthy vs. unhealthy intimate relationships
- Members will address reawakening sexuality
- Members will learn to embrace their own body image

Group Content:

On the Board: Since defining Sex is a clarifying place to begin, the first activity for the group begins with the facilitator writing on the board the question "What is Sex?".

Discussion: Members are invited to explore the many and varied definition of sex. A list of responses are written on the board and processed with the group.

The Facilitator should then introduce the topic of consent and guide the group discussion regarding the definition and nature of consent as it relates to healthy sexuality and equity in an intimate relationship. Members can be asked to write their definitions of consent and then share answers with the group.

On the Board: Facilitator writes "Sexual Ground Rules To Make Me Feel Safe"

Discussion: Because their own personal boundaries were breached, many survivors do not really understand that they can set healthy boundaries with current or future intimate partners in order to regain the sense of sexual control they may feel they have lost. Note: The facilitator can solicit those rules from members to write on the board. Facilitator may also choose to ask group members whether they feel comfortable with the facilitator writing those rules on the board or whether members would prefer to write their own and then share selected ground rules and boundaries in group processing.

Members should then be given the handout entitled "Healthy vs Unhealthy Relationships" (See Appendix B, Week 9) which compares the two. The group can then process and learn how to recognize the differences between healthy and unhealthy intimate relationships and discuss how to spot red flags that may trigger members to remember past abuse.

Activity: Members are given the handout entitled "Keys to Reawaken Your Sexuality" (See Appendix B, Week 9). Facilitator should lead members in discussing alternative holistic therapies that can aid them in their journey towards sexual healing and how their sensuality can be cultivated. Members are invited to share any of their activities or therapies that have helped them. Members will also be given a handout to fill in and explore how they feel about their body image, the parts they like and dislike, and how to embrace and love the totality of who they are as physical entities.

Session Wrap-Up: The session will end with the facilitator conducting a deep breathing exercise to relax and ground members. The empowering affirmation to be spoken in unison to end the session: "I am a sexual being and honor a healthy sexuality as my birthright."

Potential Challenges:

The facilitator must be cognizant of the fact that some group members may not be ready to make the changes necessary to foster sexual healing. If they feel obligated or forced to process the topic when they are not ready, those feelings of resistance may unconsciously trigger memories of their abuse and negatively impact the sexual healing they are actively seeking.

Group members must be encouraged to participate in the group session and process the information when they feel ready to do so – not because they feel they "should" in order to please the facilitator. The facilitator can frame the information as an adventure, exploration, or self-discovery. Those choices will allow members to empower themselves by utilizing their own time table in an ongoing journey towards sexual health.

Homework:

Members are encouraged to journal in order to explore and compare their past sexual attitudes against the new information processed in Week 9. Members are also asked to think about implementing one healing option from the "Keys To Awakening Your Sexuality" handout sheet.

CHAPTER 13

Week 10: Building Self-Esteem

Philosophy and Foundation:

The Chinese philosopher Lao Tse wrote: "Care about other people's approval and you will be their prisoner."

A healthy self-esteem implies that you accept, respect, trust, and believe in yourself. You appreciate the unique person you are and know what you think, feel, and want. You can live comfortably with your personal strengths and weaknesses without undo self-criticism. When self-esteem is low, that deficiency creates an emptiness that one tries to fill with external validation from others.

Unfortunately, sexual assault survivors not only experience emotional and physical pain, but their self-esteem has been damaged as well.

Learning Objectives:

- To identify where self-esteem is developed
- To explore some of the causes of low self-esteem
- To learn how survivors sabotage their own self-esteem
- To recognize the 10 strategies for building self-esteem
- To add positive affirmations to one's daily life that are esteem-boosting

Group Content:

On the Board: Facilitator should ask the group the question: "What is self-esteem?" and put those definitions on the board. Then below or next to the definitions, facilitator should draw a line on the board (can either be vertical or horizontal), with the numbers 1 through 10 and ask group members to identify where they think their own personal self-esteem is on this continuum *today*.

Discussion: The fundamental truth is that self-esteem comes from within, and it does not develop overnight. It is built gradually through a person's exposure and willingness to achieve successes in many areas of their life. And this exposure and learning begins in childhood with our first caretakers. It is important to recognize that sometimes, we have had to be the nurturing loving parent to ourselves that we did not have as children for a variety of reasons.

Questions for facilitator to ask include "What messages did you get from your parents?" "Is it okay to compliment yourself?" "Were you loved unconditionally?" and "Were you rewarded or punished for being assertive and having boundaries?"

Discussion: Should include the points that not having a voice as a child creates problems for the adult who cannot voice his/her needs and boundaries which, in some cases, contributed to one's victimization. Also, not being allowed to be proud of accomplishments creates the negative self-esteem in adults where nothing is good enough.

On the Board: Facilitator should write "Some Reasons for Low Self-Esteem" and let group members contribute their own reasons. Among them should be: overly critical parents, parental abuse/neglect, parental rejection, parental over-protectiveness or hovering, significant childhood losses/trauma.

Discussion: Since parental or primary caretakers' comments contribute greatly to low self-esteem, the survivor then continues the pattern with negative self-talk. Facilitator should direct members to think/look back at Week 6 and identify some of the Trolls of Limited Thinking that impact them through negative self-talk. This negative self-talk is indicative of the four personality types that develop: The Worrier, The Critic, The Victim, and The Perfectionist.

On the Board: Facilitator should write the four personality types and then the names of the Trolls that contribute to poor self-esteem. Among them should be:

- The Worrier – Catastrophizing, Magnifying, Awfulizing (This is terrible and you're causing it to be even worse!)
- The Critic – Filtering, Personalizing (You can't do anything right!)
- The Victim -- Personalizing, Over-generalizing, Emotional Reasoning (You are helpless, powerless!)
- The Perfectionist – Polarized Thinking, The Shoulds (Everything has to be perfect or it is not acceptable!) See Appendix B, Week 10 for a starter list of the Most Common and Unreasonable Shoulds. Facilitator can ask group members to add their own personal "Shoulds" to the list.

Discussion: Centers around the ones with which group members personally identify and why. Facilitator can then ask the group member "What other way can you look at this that will add to your self-esteem instead of take away from it?"

Handout: Facilitator should distribute the handout "Ten Strategies for Building Self-Esteem" with a nod to the University of Texas at Austin (See Appendix B, Week 10). As the Facilitator goes over each strategy, group members should be directed to add one change they can make in their life that will improve their self-esteem in this area. For example:

1. Free yourself from the Shoulds. *What "should" can you release that will give you more time, peace, feeling of being in control?*
2. Respect your own needs. *What personal need can you identify that will give you a greater feeling of happiness and fulfillment?*

3. Set achievable goals & experience success. *When you constantly set the bar higher without appreciating what you have achieved, you never feel good enough. In what area of your life can you just say "I did this well!" or "Thank you!" and enjoy the moment?*

4. Take risks. *This is a tough one for survivors, but it is necessary for healing from assault and living a happier life. What little/large risk can you take that will give you more freedom?*

5. Make decisions. *What decision have you been avoiding making because you felt you did not have the right, strength, or self-esteem to make? So what if you are wrong? You will have learned from that and can move on to make better decisions next time!*

6. Solve problems. *The more you avoid problems you can solve, the more you undermine your self-esteem. As before, it does not matter if the result is perfect or one you can build on; the important thing is to increase your skill levels and solving problems is one of those skills.*

7. Develop your skills. *There is nothing like learning something new to increase a person's confidence. What skill/thing have you been putting off learning that you can implement in your life?*

8. Emphasize your strengths. *Think back to Week 4 and consult your Strengths list. What is one strength in particular of which you are proud?*

9. Rely on your own opinion of yourself – not anyone else's! *Only you know what you have been through, surmounted or achieved. Why would you internalize anyone else's opinion? Write down one thing you really admire about yourself.*

10. Talk to yourself positively – not negatively. *At the end of each of these units, we have included a positive affirmation. What positive affirmation can you say to yourself each morning, noon and night that will increase your self-esteem?*

Optional Activity: Depending on the time left or Facilitator's preparation, Facilitator can lead group in creating a page of self-affirmations with each person listing one, or find and distribute a page of affirmations that group members can take home.

Session Wrap-Up: Facilitator can lead group in deep breathing exercise. Positive affirmation to be said in unison – "I am learning to love all the parts of me!"

Potential Challenges:

This unit is fairly benign and continues the process of building on each member's view of him/herself. One challenge may be a member decompensating as thoughts of a particularly cruel comment from childhood, or reaction to one's sexual assault disclosure overpowers a member.

A more common challenge is that, in giving the Homework assignment (below) and articulating that there are only two more weeks of Group, Facilitators may get some resistance from members who have difficulty with termination. This is something that will need to be addressed in this and the last two sessions. It is important to allow members to express their feelings. For many, this group is the only time a member has felt comfortable/accepted after disclosing sexual abuse or assault and they may be reluctant to see it come to an end.

IMPORTANT - Homework:

This homework assignment is being given two weeks ahead of time so group members have time to think about and compile it. Facilitator should distribute handout labeled "Medicine Bundle" See Annex B, Week 10). Facilitator can ask the following questions and describe the Medicine Bundle: What totem inspires you? What gives you strength when you hold it or look at it during times of stress? What item helps you through the tough times or gives you a feeling of power?

Derived from the medicine rituals of the Native Americans, the Medicine Bundle is comprised of symbolic articles and/or written words that inspire power and healing. In the Native American culture, the Medicine Bundle was considered the most holy of holies – and each was a reflection of the young brave who put it together.

Members should be directed to make their own Medicine Bundles comprised of nor more than 3-5 objects (depending on the size of the group) that they will bring in to share in the last session. These objects can range from photos, jewelry given by significant person in the survivor's life, or objects they have accumulated at important junctures of their life.

CHAPTER 14

Week 11: Mourning Your Losses and Moving On

Philosophy and Foundation:

The mantra of those in 12-step programs is "the first step to recovery is admitting you have a problem."

An important step in healing from sexual violence is to validate that trauma. A complete life is never sorrow free. The road to acceptance of any tragedy in life's ups and downs begins with getting in touch with one's sadness so that one can validate and mourn losses and move on.

For sexual assault survivors, recovery is a spiral process rather than a linear one and wherever they are in that process, must be honored. The spectrum of recovery and healing may go from victim to survivor to "thriver" and back again at different times. For those survivors assaulted as children, the interruption in an important developmental process often means a loss of innocence, trust, and childhood experiences. The grief process involves compassion and sympathy both from the survivors and from the people around them.

Thus, taking the time to name and mourn their losses can provide the validation necessary to successfully moving on to a healthier emotional life..

Learning Objectives:

- To guide members in naming and recording their losses, suffered due to sexual violence
- To explore the issues of vulnerability versus empowerment
- To encourage the validation, acceptance and integration of trauma events into members' lives
- To understand that external traumatic events do not define who a person is as an individual
- To break the pattern of getting stuck in the cycle of trauma and grief

Group Content:

On the Board: Facilitator writes "Losses I Have Experienced" and distributes handout that group members can fill in (See Appendix B, Week 11). Members can use the Circle of Life handout from Week 4 as a guide if needed as they list the many losses their sexual abuse caused in their lives.

After giving members time to write out their losses (10 minutes or so), the facilitator should ask group members to share some of these losses. They can be written on the board so that members can experience the universality of their trauma. Some of the losses can include: lost opportunities, faith, trust, family ties and relationships, lost innocence, finances and safety.

Facilitator can process these losses with members, asking:

- If their healing has been worth the journey and suggesting that reliving painful memories and experiencing loss are part of the healing process;
- How growth has developed from the trauma;
- If they can identify a particular epiphany that may have resulted from their personal catastrophe that has helped them to move on.

Discussion: As the Facilitator looks at termination the following week, it is important to articulate this and encourage group members to acknowledge and process how far they have come by identifying three things they are proud of achieving over the past ten sessions. Facilitator can list these responses on the board in order to validate members' ego strength and resilience. Members should be encouraged to discuss how moving on from the sexual violence and abuse and regaining their power to live a full life is the best revenge against an offender, as well as an antidote to the grief caused by the trauma.

On the Board: Facilitator writes "Things I Like About Myself Now"

Discussion: Facilitator encourages each member to process and contribute some things they like about themselves in order to separate the trauma from who they are as individuals. Survivors may list personal attributes, close relationships, abilities, and achievements.

Termination Preparation: It is important not to overlook this aspect of coming to the end of the group. Group members have likely bonded with each other as they have shared some of the most intimate details of their lives. Facilitator can refer to Irvin Yalom's 11 Therapeutic Factors of Group Therapy (See Annex B, Week 11), or simply ask group members to process how they feel about the group ending the following week.

Session Wrap-Up: Facilitator can lead group in deep breathing exercise. The empowering affirmation they can speak in unison: "I now let go of my sorrow and choose to accept and love myself!"

Potential Challenges:

There are two potential challenges to be faced in Week 11.

First, a group member's grief may be so deep-seated that clinical depression and despondency cripple the ability to heal and accept the trauma. Continually buying into "victim hood" may give some members the idea that they will always be powerless. By resisting their own higher selves, they may tend to be re-victimized.

Also, if a member is forced to continually interact with their abuser, or family or friends that have protected an abuser, the healing process can also be negatively impacted. The Facilitator must be alert to a member who exhibits an inability to process the concept of mourning and grief along with the resulting paralysis that occurs when members continue to see themselves as victims. Additional processing may be necessary in individual therapy.

Second, because the termination of the group is now fully explored and out on the table, the Facilitator may see some expressions of anger over "abandonment" as well as some members becoming withdrawn and incommunicative. Again, these clients may need to be referred for additional individual counseling in order to deal with the underlying issues.

Homework:

As part of the strategy of acceptance and integration during the mourning process, group members are encouraged to create a time line -- in chronological order—of all their significant life events from birth until the present, until all of the member's significant memories have been recorded. Traumatic memories along with other life events such as graduations, first dates, marriage, moving to new home, etc. can provide some perspective for the member. The activity provides a more realistic portrait of the context of a survivor's life and narrows the focus on a specific trauma.

Group members are also reminded to bring their Medicine Bundles to share with the group for the closing session.

CHAPTER 15

Week 12: The Pursuit of Happiness & Group Termination

Philosophy and Foundation:

Wisdom comes only when you stop looking for it and start living the life the Creator intended for you. Hopi Indian Proverb

Life may provide the building lot, but we build the structure. By becoming our own architect, we also have the capacity to become the heroes in our own life stories.

How to gain, keep, and recover happiness is, in fact, the underlying motive of all we do and all we are willing to endure. For sexual assault survivors recovering from trauma, happiness and pleasure are signs that healing is taking place.

The factors that correlate with happiness such as self-esteem, peace of mind, healthy habits, optimism, mastery and control are the same as those which help treat post-traumatic stress disorder. As survivors move along the spectrum of healing and move to a place of peace and acceptance, they can begin to realize that happiness is a choice – not just a stroke of luck – but the consequences of personal effort.

Learning Objectives:

- To share the items that empower each member
- To process the journey towards the pursuit of happiness
- To affirm and celebrate personal growth
- To terminate the group counseling relationship in a healthy manner

Group Content:

Activity – Group members share their individual Medicine Bundles, introducing each totem and explaining its significance to the member. As members process the items that give them strength and power, the Facilitator affirms and validates that each member's identity is not simply wrapped up in the trauma, but is part of a larger story that includes the selected totems and the people who gave them.

Discussion: Once all the Medicine Bundles are shared, the Facilitator points out that while trauma is part of their life stories and they will honor their history as survivors, they can also cultivate the other strong, resilient parts of themselves that make up the complete individual.

On the Board: Facilitator writes "Things That Will Facilitate My Happiness"

Members will list factors that correlate with happiness as facilitator writes those on the board and processes with the group. Factors for discussion may include rewarding activities, an optimistic attitude, healthy habits, positive interpersonal relationships, heightened self-esteem, and active involvement in life.

Handout: Members will be given a handout entitled "The Three M's" (See Appendix B, Week 12) illustrating how the pursuit of happiness can be distilled down to: Meditation (self-awareness / contemplation), Moderation (overcoming obsessive unhealthy behavior), and Motivation (planning and reaching healthy goals). The group will process how each initiative, if practiced consistently, can lead to positive life changes.

Discussion: A final discussion of Termination. Facilitator should ask members to explore and process their feelings around the significance of "endings" in their lives. As they review the group experience, members will discuss how it has impacted their journey towards growth and self-actualization.

Post Test: In order to measure members' emotional scale after exposure to the 12 week psycho-educational group curriculum, the Facilitator should distribute the DASS (Depression / Anxiety / Stress Scale) again as a post test for members to fill out before the end of session. Post termination, the facilitator can compare members' pre-test emotional baseline scores to those after exposure to the group format. The DASS measurement tool (along with any intervening variables) may also serve to quantify the effectiveness of the facilitator in his / her ability to effect change. Members will also be given a Group Participant Evaluation form to measure the effectiveness of the group format.

Graduation: To end the session, the Facilitator should distribute the inspirational "diploma" (See Appendix B, Week 12) to each member that reaffirms the member's healing journey.

Session Wrap-Up: The facilitator should conduct a final deep breathing exercise followed by an empowering affirmation spoken in unison: "I am the hero in my own life story!"

Potential Challenges:

Even though the psycho-educational group format has a finite beginning and ending, the termination process can still be both poignant and painful for group members. Since the format is a closed group, members have gotten to know each other over the 12 week cycle and through sharing their traumas, may have grown close. Although some members may want to continue the relationships with group members after termination, others may not, so feelings of rejection and abandonment could develop.

Termination may also sadden some members who are not comfortable with "endings" of any kind. They may experience a sense of loss and fear they will regress without the group experience to empower them. The facilitator must be aware of the group's emotional temperature during the termination session so that he / she can process members' feelings based on the meaning of endings.

Homework:

In a final assignment, the Facilitator should encourage group members to utilize the knowledge gained during the 12 week group experience, and continue to work on their own personal growth as survivors – making the decision to heal every day.

CHAPTER 16

A Final Word to Therapists About Self-Care

"Knowing others is intelligence. Knowing yourself is true wisdom.
Mastering others is strength. Mastering yourself is true power."
Tao Te Ching

Childhood abuse….gang rape…partner violence….date rape….incest. None of these stories of human tragedy and violence are easy for a clinician to hear daily and process.

Although we hope our positive influence will impact the client, *their* influence often impacts us. As empathic professionals, we may discover we have internalized their pain and experienced vicarious trauma and secondary post traumatic stress.

Many clinicians not trained in the dynamics of sexual assault may choose not to process a client's personal disclosure of sexual violence and will swiftly refer a survivor to a trauma specialist. This is a viable alternative and will ultimately be in the best interests of the client.

For those who choose empathic engagement with a client's trauma story, the experience of vicarious trauma can often be functionally disruptive as well as psychologically destabilizing, resulting in an accumulation of negative psychic energy that can impact the clinician's inner life. The clinician can be infected with a patient's sadness; a condition Jung called "psychic poisoning." The term "vicarious traumatization" has been utilized more frequently after the events of September 11, 2001.

Therapists can suffer emotional depletion, a feeling of isolation when working long hours and within the confines of increasing laws governing patient confidentiality, and even an inability to shut off the "counseling face." Counter-transference issues may arise that lead to over-identification with the client as he or she adopts the role of rescuer, parent, or guardian.

In cases where the clinician has a personal history of sexual abuse, the counter-transference may be more pronounced if the therapist has not fully worked through his/her own victimization. In those situations, there is often a danger that the clinician may be triggered by their own traumatic memories and may be at risk for getting their trauma histories mixed up with their clients'.

Many therapists who work with survivors of sexual abuse every day find that it is common to occasionally feel overwhelmed, even if the clinician is highly trained and competent. It is therefore essential that clinicians who choose to do this vital work with survivors of sexual violence are extremely mindful in addressing their own self-care and nurturing so that they can not only make a positive impact on their clients, but also serve as role models for healthy and well balanced living.

A long term action plan to help you deal with vicarious trauma begins with being aware and mindful of what you are experiencing so that you can begin to understand your reactions.

How often do *you* do the following?

- Check in with yourself regularly and notice if some information is making you uncomfortable, stressed, or tired.
- Take time to reflect on any discomfort and utilize holistic tools to get in touch with yourself such as journaling, painting, drawing, and talking to someone you trust.
- Develop a strategy to balance challenging with less challenging clients and tasks in your daily schedule.
- Within your work life, be mindful of taking breaks for meals, rest, and some physical activity. Stop work after a reasonable number of hours; emotionally exhausted workers can actually do more harm than good especially in disaster response situations.
- Establish rituals that indicate a clear separation between work and play each day, developing after-work patterns that remind you that work is over and that decompressing when you get home is essential to your emotional and physical balance. It can be as simple as changing your work clothes as soon as you get home and going for a walk, to the gym or a yoga class; making a healthy dinner; reading the latest chapter in the book you've been meaning to finish; getting out in nature; practicing deep breathing and meditation; or simply taking a "time out" when you need it
- Take time for spiritual renewal in order to rediscover purpose and joy, keep up with your professional development, and connect to friends, family and community on a regular basis.

The keystone of a therapist's self-care is ultimately creating that healthy balance between your work life and your personal life where the demands of the work do not overpower the need for personal self-nurturing. If your own battery feels drained, you cannot help others charge theirs and recover equilibrium.

Listed below are some self-nurturing ideas you can utilize in your on-going journey towards a healthy work-life balance and self-care. See how many of these coping strategies you can integrate into your daily life. Feel free to add your own to the list!

Spend time with loved ones
Go on nature walks / hikes
Sit on the beach
Go fishing
Create a healthy nutrition plan
Practice deep breathing exercises
Go to a Yoga class
Get a gym membership – and use it!
Write in a journal
Read a good book

Watch movie marathons
Relax in front of a lit fireplace
Commit to one Tech-free day a week
Indulge in Sunday afternoon naps
Make a Spirituality commitment
Practice meditation / mindfulness
Take up photography
Do an art project / crafting/ Scrapbooking
Get a free makeover
Get a great haircut
Go for a manicure / pedicure
Get a massage
Take a bubble bath by candlelight
Go for a sauna
Plan a Spa day
Watch a sunrise / sunset
Visit the zoo
Have breakfast in bed
Visit a museum
Go to the opera
Buy Concert tickets
Take up cooking /baking
Decorate
Go shoe shopping
Socialize with friends
Play with pets
Plan a holiday
Go to bed early
Dance with yourself
Listen to favorite tunes
Write your own song
Go camping
Bike ride
Horseback ride
Learn a sport
Learn to play an instrument
Buy yourself flowers
Think happy thoughts

Finally, give yourself permission to experience success and feel good about the work you are doing. It may be difficult, but you *are* changing lives.

ABOUT THE AUTHORS

Denise Lang-Grant is a licensed therapist specializing in sexual and other traumas and author of nine other non-fiction books on family relationships, health, and true crime. Former Director of Atlantic Health's rape crisis center in Morris County, New Jersey, she is the state facilitator for strengthening community response to military survivors of sexual violence and also serves as an adjunct instructor for Seton Hall University's Master's in Counseling program. Denise maintains a private practice in Morris and Somerset counties and was a major contributor to the inaugural edition of the first encyclopedia to deal with sexual trauma and recovery. She is a member of the American Counseling Association and the American Academy of Experts in Traumatic Stress. Denise and her husband Alan Grant, a musician/songwriter, live in Somerset County with their two dogs. Denise can be reached at dvlwords@gmail.com

Irene Colucci Lebbad is a licensed clinical social worker with extensive background in sexual abuse, domestic violence, and behavioral health. A former director of the Somerset County NJ Sexual Assault Support Services program, she is currently one of the principles in a group practice specializing in sexual violence and abuse. Through more than 10 years as a clinician working with survivors of sexual violence, incest, and abuse, Irene developed a keen understanding of how trauma from sexual abuse impacts a survivor's quality of life. She continues to conduct trainings and workshops for community organizations, law enforcement, and other professionals in order to educate and raise awareness. Irene and her husband Tom have a large extended family and live in Somerset County New Jersey. Irene can be reached at Irene.Lebbad@gmail.com

A P P E N D I X   A

GROUP FORMS

℘ 12 WEEK GROUP CURRICULUM:

WEEK 1 – Breaking The Silence: Our Stories, Who We Are

WEEK 2 – Dealing With PTSD or Why Am I Not Myself?

WEEK 3 – Understanding That It Wasn't Your Fault!

WEEK 4 – How The Assault Changed your Life

WEEK 5 – Coping Mechanisms and Survival Skills

WEEK 6- The 9 Trolls of Limited Thinking

WEEK 7 – Anger, The Backbone of Healing

WEEK 8 – Developing Your Support System

WEEK 9 –Healing Sexually

WEEK 10 – Building Self-Esteem

WEEK 11 – Mourning Your Losses and Moving On

WEEK 12 – The Pursuit of Happiness and Group Termination

℘ GROUP MEMBER REGISTRATION

NAME: _____

ADDRESS: _____

TELEPHONE: _____

DATE OF BIRTH: _____ AGE: _____

EMAIL: _____

EMERGENCY CONTACT: _____

RELATIONSHIP TO GROUP MEMBER: _____

CELL PHONE: _____

REFERRED BY: _____

THERAPIST (If applicable): _____

THERAPIIST'S PHONE: _____

DEMOGRAPHIC INFORMATION:

WAS THERE A POLICE REPORT? YES _____ NO _____

ARE YOU CURRENTLY EMPLOYED? YES _____ NO _____

ARE YOU A COLLEGE STUDENT? YES _____ NO _____

DO YOU HAVE A DISABILITY? YES _____ NO _____

ETHNICITY (Optional): _____

CONFIDENTIALITY AGREEMENT

All group sessions are confidential. Group members, like the leaders, are bound ethically not to disclose the contents of group sessions. Groups are private and confidential at all times. Member's disclosures are not shared outside of the group.

- I agree to respect the confidentiality and privacy of all group members regarding any and all personal disclosures within the group.
- At no time will I disclose any personal information from group members to anyone outside of the group.
- I will agree that all group discussions will remain confidential and within the confines of the group.

*EXCEPTIONS TO CONFIDENTIALITY:

In the case where a member reports child abuse, suicidality or homicidality, the facilitator is bound by law and ethics to notify the proper authorities. The facilitator will make every effort to work with the member during this process.

_____

Member's Signature and Name Printed

_____

Date

GROUP GROUND RULES

- Start on time, end on time

- What is said in Group, stays in Group

- Be honest and demonstrate respect for others

- Use "I" statements rather than "you" or "they"

- No group discussion about a member unless he/she is present

- Share one at a time, respecting one another's efforts

- No monopolizing Group time

- No verbal attacks on another member for his/her opinion

- No inappropriate touching

- No socializing outside of Group sessions

- NO drugs or alcohol

- Call or Text facilitators beforehand if unable to attend group

℘ GROUP MEMBER SELF-ASSESSMENT

Note: Use this self- assessment to determine your strengths and weaknesses as a Group member. Circle the answer that best fits you at the start of this group.

1. I am open to trusting others in a group setting. Yes   No   Maybe

2. Others tend to trust me in a group setting. Yes   No   Maybe

3. I am comfortable disclosing personal and meaningful information to group members. Yes   No   Maybe

4. I am willing to formulate goals as applies to group. Yes   No   Maybe

5. I am generally an active participant, as opposed to being an observer. Yes   No   Maybe   NA

6. I am willing to opening express my feelings about, and reactions to, what is occurring in the group. Yes   No   Maybe   NA

7. I listen attentively to what others are saying and am able to discern more than the obvious content of what is said. Yes   No   Maybe

8. I do not give in to group pressure by doing or saying things that do not seem right to me or are in conflict with my values. Yes   No   Maybe

9. I am able to give direct and honest feedback to other group members, and I am open to receiving feedback about my statements and behavior from other members without being resentful. Yes   No   Maybe

10. I prepare myself for the group session by thinking of what I want from that experience and what I am willing to do to achieve those goals. Yes   No   Maybe

11. While I take an active part in the group, I avoid monopolizing the conversation. Yes   No   Maybe

12. I avoid storytelling by describing what I am experiencing in the moment. Yes   No   Maybe

13. I consider myself a supportive person and am able to support other group members when it is appropriate. Yes   No   Maybe

14. I am able to confront others in a direct and caring manner by letting them know how I am affected by them Yes   No   Maybe

A P P E N D I X   B

GROUP HANDOUTS

WHO ARE WE?

Please select a partner from the group. Interview that person and then use this information to introduce him/her to the rest of the Group.

- YOUR NAME:

- WHERE DO YOU LIVE?

- WHAT DO YOU DO TO RELAX?

- WHAT IS YOUR FAVORITE RESTAURANT?

- DO YOU HAVE ANY PETS?

- DO YOU HAVE ANY TALENTS / HOBBIES?

- WHAT DO YOU LIKE BEST ABOUT YOURSELF?

- HOW DO YOU THINK THIS GROUP WILL BENEFIT YOU?

- WHAT IS SOMETHING THAT YOU WOULD LIKE EVERYONE TO KNOW ABOUT YOU?

THE MYTHS ABOUT SEXUAL ASSAULT

1. Sexual assault is a crime of passion.

2. You can easily identify sexual offenders.

3. Strangers commit the highest percentage of rapes.

4. If you stay out of deserted alleys and other isolated places, you should be safe from sexual violence.

5. A victim has to say "No" for it to legally be considered a sexual assault.

6. You can identify rape survivors by their massive physical injuries.

7. Women lie about rape as an act of revenge or guilt.

8. It is virtually impossible for a male to be raped.

9. Gay men represent the greatest danger to boys and other males regarding sexual violence and abuse.

10. If a male or female victim's body responds or reaches orgasm during a sexual assault, it means that the victim was enjoying the act and it is, therefore, consensual.

11. The number of alleged victims recanting proves that nothing happened and the report of a sexual assault was false.

WHY DISCLOSE?

Disclosing your abuse can be frightening, but can also be very empowering - serving to validate your experience and giving you some control over it as well. Listed below are some reasons that may speak to you:

- It liberates me from keeping a secret

- It allows me to get in touch with complex feelings of guilt, shame, and anger

- It fosters validation of the trauma I have experienced

- It allows me to move forward and reclaim my life

- It facilitates the beginning of moving away from victim-hood

- It opens the door to support and healing

- It serves as a testimony to my ego-strength and resiliency in survivorship

- It gives me an opportunity to expose my abuser

- It will no longer isolate me from others with the same experience

- It allows me to engage people who are empathic to my story

- It helps me to address the reasons for my depression and anxiety

- It can help me become emotionally stronger

STRESS MANAGEMENT TECHNIQUES

The Square Belly Breath

1. Find a comfortable position
2. Close your eyes, or leave them open, focusing on a spot on the floor
3. Focus your attention on your breath
4. As you breathe in, allow your abdominal muscles to rise
5. Fill your lungs to capacity on the inhale
6. As you breathe out, let your abdominal muscles fall, breathing out completely
7. On the inhale, count 1-2-3-4
8. On the exhale, count 4-3-2-1

Mantra Breathing

1. Find your comfortable position
2. Close your eyes, or leave them open, focusing on a spot on the floor
3. Continue abdominal breathing as above
4. On the inhale, repeat the words "I am"
5. On the exhale, repeat the word "Re-laxed"
6. Repeat exercise at least 6 times

Symptoms of Rape Trauma Syndrome

The term encompasses the emotional, physical and behavioral stress reactions that result from facing a life-threatening situation or an event perceived as life-threatening to oneself or loved ones. As a result of the trauma, there are a series of reactions and feeling that follow. They can include:

- Shock
- Numbing
- Inability to concentrate
- Fear
- Guilt
- Nightmares
- Suicidal thoughts and feelings
- Not knowing who to trust
- Depression
- Doubting one's self and judgement
- Disorientation and/or confusion
- Interruptions of daily routine by flashbacks
- Anxiety
- Self-blame
- Sleep disturbances
- Eating disruption or disorders
- Feelings of betrayal
- Shame

Reactions to the trauma can be manifested in two styles:

- Expressive – The survivor demonstrates her/his feelings of anxiety, fear, anger, etc. through crying, restlessness, tension or even laughter.
- Controlled – The survivor is calm, composed, subdued.

These are natural reactions to an abnormal event. Help in minimizing these symptoms and adopting healthy coping skills can be achieved through counseling.

✐ ABUSE AND YOUR EMOTIONS – MAKING THE CONNECTION

- Every emotional reaction to an event has a *purpose*!
- It's entirely normal to experience feelings more intensely when you begin to face situations you've been avoiding for a long time. This group work may dig those feelings up...that is part of cleaning out the wound.
- Now if and when you're finally able to really think about why you felt the way you did when you were abused, your emotions suddenly begin to make sense.
- Too often however, survivors focus on their emotions but ignore the positive message that lies beneath. A part of healing involves listening to yourself.
- Remember, your emotional symptoms are simply a reaction to what happened to you, but you can learn to use them in a way that helps you grow.
- So I would like to help you increase your awareness of your feelings, and give you some tools for identifying and expressing them more readily.....

SOME FACTS ABOUT FEELINGS:

1. *Your entire body is affected by your feelings*. The nervous system and brain are both involved resulting in somatic symptoms such as elevated heart rate, sweating, and shaking.

2. *Your thoughts impact your feelings as well*. Your emotional reactions are based on your thoughts at the time. Realizing the connection can help alter your perception into a more realistic rationale.

3. *Your feelings will energize you*. Own your feelings and work with them so you can become more self-aware and energetic. Suppressed feelings can fester and cause depression and anxiety among other issues.

4. *Your feelings can influence others.* Working with and understanding your own feelings first will help; you not to take on the burden of someone else's emotional reactions.

5. *Your feelings are not quantified.* Right or wrong, they are simply reactions. You have a right to own your feelings whatever they may be. Just be cognizant of the perceptions that led you to experience them in the first place.

6. ***Repressing your feelings may be unhealthy.*** Although acknowledging our feelings can be painful, constantly suppressing them will eventually lead to the inability to identify, understand, and express them fully.

SO WHY DO WE SUPPRESS OUR FEELINGS?

1. ***We were not in control at the time of our abuse.*** So the need to maintain control thereafter becomes paramount, including control of our feelings. Denying them consistently serves to reinforce our fear of somehow "losing it"
2. ***Growing up with overly critical parents can force us to rein in our true feelings.*** The inability to express ourselves fully as children often leads to suppression of our feelings as adults. Feelings of anger are most common because as children, we were not allowed to express that emotion. Punishment for angry outbursts were frequently enforced.

SO HOW DO WE LEARN TO OWN OUR FEELINGS?

1. ***ACKNOWLEDGE THEM.*** Name the feeling, validate the symptoms, and feel what's going on in your body. Utilize meditation and relaxation techniques to focus.
2. ***EXPRESS THEM.*** Expressing your feelings can prove to be a cathartic experience. Journaling, processing in therapy, disclosing to someone close that you trust, and engaging in creative endeavors can raise awareness.
3. ***CONVEY THEM.*** To the appropriate people who caused those feelings to manifest.

✒ CHALLENGING YOUR CRITICAL INNER VOICE: THE FUEL FOR SHAME AND GUILT

My critical inner voice tells me:

_____
_____
_____
_____
_____
_____
_____
_____
_____
_____
_____
_____
_____

The reality tells me:

_____
_____
_____
_____
_____
_____
_____
_____
_____
_____
_____
_____

REALITY TESTING FEELINGS OF SHAME AND GUILT

Guilt and shame are the enemies that paralyze you. Guilt keeps you "stuck" so that growth cannot happen – it is the poison that kills the plant. So let's begin to think rationally about where guilt belongs and where the fault really lies in your trauma story.

Write down your truth and validate yourself by listing why you are blameless:

Why it's not my fault

_____

Why it's not my fault

_____

Why it's not my fault

_____

Why it's not my fault

_____

Why it's not my fault

_____

Why it's not my fault

_____

Why it's not my fault

_____

FINDING OUR STRENGTHS

Definition of "Strength": the quality or state of being strong : capacity for exertion or endurance; the power to resist force : <u>SOLIDARITY</u>, <u>TOUGHNESS</u>: power of resisting attack. (Merriam Webster Dictionary)

When you look at the negative effects of abuse in your life, it's hard to imagine that you could have developed strengths at the same time. But we all do develop strengths. Recognizing your strengths does not mean you have to minimize your abuse or discount the negative effects it has had on your life.

Recognizing your strengths is a way to feel good about yourself and despite what has happened to you! It is a way to recognize the abilities and qualities that allow you to heal.

Look at this list and put a check next to statements that apply to you. You can also add others:

1. I am stubborn. I won't give up!
2. I won't let anybody abuse me anymore!
3. I have empathy for other people in pain.
4. I understand human suffering.
5. I am a realist; I can figure out how things really are.
6. If I lived through abuse, I can live through anything.
7. I am more self-sufficient; I can take care of myself.
8. I have courage.
9. I know how to handle a crisis.
10. I am calm and patient.
11. I have learned what makes a good friend.
12. I am a good listener.
13. _____
14. _____

Fun Activity: Print Your Name and for every letter in your name, list a strength or something positive.

For example:

Cindy = Caring
            Intelligent
            Nice to others
            Yes, I can!

Now, it is your turn. First, print your name:
_____

 YOUR WHEEL OF LIFE

What was impacted/changed by your assault/abuse?

Optional areas to include: Spirituality, Education, Emotional Well-Being
Write the changes in the pie wedges. Then consider the strengths
you have developed *because* of the trauma.

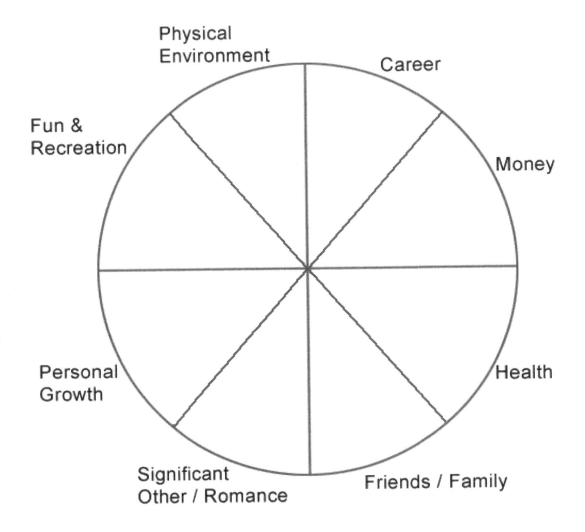

ℓ IDENTIFYING YOUR COPING MECHANISMS

This list represents some of the most utilized coping mechanisms for survivors. Check the ones that you identify with and add some of your own.

Suppressing feelings

Intellectualizing

Gambling

Sleeping too much

Emotionally disconnecting

Isolating

Hyper-vigilance

Eating compulsively

Substance abuse

Eating disorders

Suicidal ideations

Obsessive Compulsive habits

Abusing others

Denial

Compulsive sex

Self-mutilation

Avoiding Sex

Insomnia

Workaholism

WAYS TO NURTURE YOURSELF

Take the time to do things that make you feel good at least once a day. It is part of the healing journey you have chosen to take. Here are some suggestions:

- Get into a great book
- Make yourself a cup of tea with honey
- Get a massage
- Go away for the weekend
- Go bike riding
- Sit in a hot tub
- Listen to great music
- Meditate
- Go to the movies
- Go to the zoo
- Buy yourself flowers
- Journal
- Paint
- Go out to dinner
- Exercise
- Use a daily affirmation
- Spend time with family and friends
- Practice Yoga

℘ Deep Breathing Meditation

Find a comfortable place to sit or lie down where you will not be disturbed.

Close your eyes if you wish.

Consciously relax your abdominal muscles and allow your abdomen to rise on the inhale and contract on the exhale.

Take in a slow, deep breath to the count of 4:

1--------------------2---------------------3--------------------4

Visualize breathing in white light, energy, and vitality.

Now exhale slowly counting:

4--------------------3---------------------2--------------------1

Visualize breathing out negative energy, toxicity, and destructive patterns.

Continue to take slow, deep breaths and be mindful of your body relaxing into a calm, peaceful state.

LET'S LIST YOUR ACCOMPLISHMENTS!

Accomplishments can be *anything* you feel proud of and could be a small
or big thing from baking a great cupcake to getting a promotion…..

_____
_____
_____
_____
_____
_____
_____
_____
_____
_____
_____
_____
_____
_____
_____
_____
_____
_____
_____
_____
_____
_____
_____

THE TROLLS OF LIMITED THINKING

These can prevent you from crossing the bridge into logical thinking:

1. **Filtering:**

2. **Polarized Thinking:**

3. **Overgeneralization:**

4. **Mind-Reading:**

5. **Catastrophizing:**

6. **Magnifying:**

7. **Personalizing:**

8. **The Shoulds:**

9. **Emotional Reasoning:**

℘ Anger Costs And Benefits

Anger is a very strong emotion and when it erupts, everyone around you gets to feel the heat. It is a healthy emotion that is often expressed in unhealthy ways. It can act as a motivator for life changes, or an inhibitor that can generate depression, rage, and intense guilt. List below how many costs and benefits of anger you can think of.

COSTS – THE BAD THINGS ABOUT ANGER	BENEFITS – THE GOOD THINGS ABOUT ANGER

How To Deal With Anger

ANGER IS A CHOICE YOU MAKE. Anger is subjective to you and your interpretation of another's behavior. Recognizing your own negative thoughts about a situation can help you change your anger into something more positive. Angry feelings that are triggered and intensified by mistaken core beliefs, could be alleviated through positive self-talk that conveys a realistic and healthy assessment of the situation, not one fueled by a negative emotional response.

BE ASSERTIVE WITH YOUR ANGER, NOT AGGRESSIVE. Communicate your frustration toward others in a manner that respects their dignity. Always use "I" statements rather than "You" statements. Pointing fingers only puts people on the defensive while "I" statements maintain respect and open the door to a dialogue, not a fight. An example: "I feel angry when you are not on time" vs. "You make me so angry when you are not on time".

YOU DON'T ALWAYS HAVE TO BE NICE. You don't have to put yourself in a position where you must be pleasing in all situations. Allow yourself to express irritation in situations when it is appropriate (ie: insults, put downs, destructive behaviors, disrespect). Direct your anger at the right person and be assertive, not aggressive with your comments. You can also journal, exercise, or use art to draw it out and discharge energy.

DON'T WORRY ABOUT ALIENATING PEOPLE YOU CARE ABOUT. Communicating angry feelings in appropriate ways to significant others is an indication that you DO care about them. If you didn't care, you would be emotionally detached and indifferent to the situation. The person you care about deserves to know where you stand on the issue in a respectful manner.

DON'T BE AFRAID OF THE "WHAT IF'S". The fear of what might happen if you let your anger out full blast is often irrational. The intensity of the emotions will diminish as soon as you allow yourself to experience them. The real danger lies in withholding for so long that to release your anger seems ominous.

LEARN TO DIFFERENTIATE VARIED LAYERS OF ANGER. If your anger is intense, you may not be ready to talk to someone yet. In that case, better to express it physically by working out, punching pillows, chopping wood, etc. When the intensity has subsided, talk it out with a neutral person first before confronting the person that generated the anger.

BRING YOUR ANGER TO A RATIONAL PLACE. Uncontrolled emotions have NO BRAIN. That's why the old cliché' of counting to ten was invented. Bringing the emotion back from your gut to a rational place in your head allows you a "cool down" period and a chance to think more clearly and analyze the issue before you move forward.

My Support System

1. Name those in your Inner Circle of Trust – that is, who do you feel you can disclose anything to, day or night, and not be judged?.
2. The Second Ring is for those who you can disclose some things, but have to edit what you say.
3. And finally, the third ring is for Everyone Else – those in your life that you have regular contact but are not trusted with your most personal information.

EVERYONE ELSE

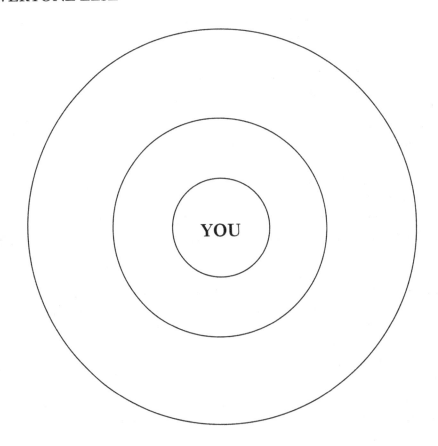

WINDOW OF TRUST

(Based on Johari Window)

#1

Things you keep
hidden about yourself
until you trust
enough to reveal

#3

Blind Spots

* Things others see but you
don't know about yourself
* Depends on feedback

#4

Unknown to you/
anyone

* Self-discovery
* Counseling
* How you will respond
to trauma

#2

Open for all to see

Window shade can
Move up and down

ℰ RECOGNIZING HEALTHY VS. UNHEALTHY RELATIONSHIPS

The following lists compare aspects of healthy and unhealthy relationship traits. Many relationships may have a combination of both. Determine if a past or current relationship is healthy so you can establish your boundaries, recognize the "red flags", and determine what you want to change.

IS IT HEALTHY?	IS IT UNHEALTHY?
Have fun together often	Gets extremely jealous and possessive
Always feel safe together	Is obsessed with the relationship
Trust each other	Puts the other person down
Are faithful to each other if you have made this commitment	Yells and treats the other like a child
Support each other's individual goals in life (like career or education)	Doesn't take the other person (or things that are important to that person) seriously.
Respect each other's opinions, even if they are different	Doesn't listen when the other talks
Solve conflicts without putting each other down	Frequently criticizes the other's friends or family
Both apologize if you're wrong	Pressures the other for sex, or makes sex hurt or feel humiliating
Both accept responsibility for your actions	Has ever threatened to hurt the other or commit suicide if they leave
Have equal decision-making power	Cheats or threatens to cheat
	Smashes, throws, or destroys things
Have some privacy (your phone, diary, letters, mail, etc. are respected as your own)	Withholds affection as a way to punish

Never feel like you're pressured for sex	Physically hurts the other
Have close friends and family like the other person and are happy for you	Embarrasses or humiliates the other
Always treat each other with respect	Plays mind games
	Uses alcohol or drugs as an excuse

ℰ REDISCOVERING YOUR SENSUAL SELF

Although many factors can contribute to a lack of sexual response, anxiety or fear due to the trauma from sexual abuse can negatively impact your sexual life. Fatigue, stress, and exhaustion due to pressures with work, money, or family can also impact and lower your sex drive.

Here are some alternative therapies that you may want to experiment with in order to regain confidence and find enjoyment in your own sexuality.

ESSENTIAL OILS:

Clary Sage, Ginger, Jasmine, Neroli, Rose, Sandalwood, and Ylang Ylang can be used in your bath to stimulate and renew your interest in sex.

BACH FLOWER REMEDIES:

Honey suckle is beneficial for those who have suffered a traumatic experience in the past such as rape or molestation. If this has led to a sense of being "dirty" and "contaminated", then Crab Apple would be beneficial. Mimulus is helpful if there is a fear of sex and Wild Rose is helpful for those who suffer from sexual ennui.

COLORS:

Meditate, wear, and surround yourself with the color orange-red. It is the color of passion, vitality, and sexual power. It is the 2nd Chakra located at the lower abdomen where sexual energy / procreation dwell. Do not confuse this red with the deep red of the 1st Chakra at the base of the spine. A blockage or imbalance in this area can make us agitated, spiteful, and bitter.

APHRODISIAC FOODS:

Chocolate, oysters, licorice, asparagus, pineapple, pomegranate, date palm, pimentos, agave, basil, cardamom, thorn apple, yams, cayenne.

HERBS:

(Women) Damiana, Kava-Kava, Ginseng, False Unicorn, Angelica, Burdock. (Men) Saw Palmetto, Yohimbe, Sassafras, Yarrow.

AROMATHERAPY:

Burn incense or candles with the following scents: Jasmine, Patchouli, Musk, Ylang Ylang, or Sandalwood.

GEMS AND STONES:

Stones associated with the 2nd Chakra are Carnelian, Opal, Sunstone, Orange Topaz. For frigidity / impotence place one of these stones on lower abdomen for 20 minutes: Alabaster, Moonstone, Sapphire, or Tourmaline. To store, wrap each stone in fine linen and place in separate boxes.

MUSIC:

Listen to any type of music that allows you to unwind – easy jazz, classical music, nature sounds, or ballad singers. We recommend that you lean towards instrumentals as lyrics sometimes trigger uncomfortable or upsetting memories.

SENSATE FOCUS:

Simply "notice" positive sensations that were pleasantly sensuous, such as the texture of your cat's fur, sinking into a warm bubble bath, the feeling when you first place your feet on the beach sand, the sensation of a cool drink on a hot day, the taste of a juicy strawberry in season. Remember, sexuality is simply one more aspect on the continuum of subtle sensations. There is a lot more to sex than just the physical part!

BODY WORK:

Dance, exercise, yoga, therapeutic massage, and sexual self-pleasuring are all ways to become more comfortable with your body. Exercise can be an appealing way for a sexual assault survivor to establish a positive sense of body awareness. Dancing can provide a positive vehicle for self-expression. Simply self-massaging your own body parts starting with a foot or a hand and working gradually over your body can help you get back in touch with your own sensual nature which is your birthright.

℘ YOUR BODY IMAGE

A wounded body cannot heal if you do not respect its needs. What are you giving your body and how is your body responding to you?

IF YOUR BODY COULD TALK, WHAT WOULD IT SAY TO YOU?

_____
_____
_____
_____
_____

WHAT PARTS OF YOUR BODY DO YOU LIKE? WHY?

_____
_____
_____
_____
_____

WHAT PARTS OF YOUR BODY DO YOU DISLIKE? WHY?

_____
_____
_____
_____
_____

WHAT ARE SOME THINGS YOU CAN DO TO HONOR YOUR BODY OVER THE NEXT WEEK?

_____
_____
_____
_____
_____

ℰ A List of the Most Common and Unreasonable *"Shoulds"*

- I *should* be the epitome of: generosity, unselfishness, consideration, courage, dignity
- I *should* be the perfect: friend, lover, parent, teacher, student, spouse
- I *should* be able to find a quick solution to every problem
- I *should* feel: happy, grateful, serene
- I *should* never feel hurt, or if I do, I should never show it
- I *should* know, understand, forsee everything
- I *should* be able to endure hardship and never complain
- I *show* never feel/show: jealousy, angery, envy, frustration
- I *should* never be tired
- I *should* never get sick
- I *should* always be a good listener
- I *should* not burden others with my problems/emotions
- I *should* love my children equally
- I *should* never make mistakes
- I *should* be self-reliant
- I *should* assert myself but never hurt anyone else's feelings

Now it is your turn. How many more "shoulds" rule your life? List them below.

THE MEDICINE BUNDLE

What totem inspires you? What gives you strength when you hold it or look at it during times of stress? What item helps you through the tough times or empowers you?

Derived from the medicine rituals of the Native Americans, the Medicine Bundle is comprised of symbolic articles and / or written words that inspire power and healing. In the Native American culture, the Medicine Bundle was considered the most holy of holies – and each was as individual as the person who created it.

If small, the medicine bundle can be worn in a pouch near the heart. If larger, it can be carried in a purse or knapsack. The contents are highly individualized but they should evoke feelings of strength, healthy inner convictions, and self-nurturance.

Examples of objects that a Medicine Bundle could contain include a photo of a supportive loved one, dried flowers or herbs from a favorite site associated with peace and safety, a piece of jewelry or scrap of clothing from a much loved relative or one who has been strongly supportive, or something symbolic of strength, such as an eagle's feather.

Homework: Your task for Week 12, the final session, is to create and bring your own personal Medicine Bundle to share with the group and to be prepared to talk about why you selected the objects you included. It can be wrapped in a small bag, towel, or handkerchief. It can be as simple or fancy as you wish. The point is to include items that inspire strength when you look at, or hold, them. Please limit your Medicine Bundle to 3-5 items.

℘ Yalom's 11 Therapeutic Factors of Group Therapy

1. Installation of hope

2. Universality

3. Imparting Information

4. Altruism

5. Corrective Recapitulation of the primary family group

6. Development of Socializing Techniques

7. Imitative Behaviors

8. Interpersonal Learning

9. Group Cohesiveness

10. Catharsis

11. Existential Factors

GRIEVING, MOURNING, AND MOVING ON

Getting in touch with the sadness over traumatic events and beginning the grief process means you're ready for the next step – Acceptance. Putting the assault in its place and making peace with the past means you can finally find the joy you deserve in the here and now.

1. *NAME YOUR LOSSES*

_____
_____
_____
_____

2. *WHY HEALING HAS BEEN WORTH IT*

_____
_____
_____
_____

3. *LIST THE THINGS YOU ARE PROUD OF*

_____
_____
_____
_____

4. *LIST THE THINGS YOU LIKE ABOUT YOURSELF*

_____
_____
_____
_____

5. *THINGS YOU DREAM ABOUT DOING IN YOUR LIFE*

_____
_____
_____

THE STAGES OF HEALING

VICTIM >	SURVIVOR >	THRIVER
Disclosure	Depression	Acceptance
The Crisis/PTSD	Anger	Integration
Shame/Guilt	Moving On	
Mourning Loss		

Recovery is a <u>*spiral*</u> *process, NOT linear. You may at times go back to an earlier stage, but each stage must be mastered over time so that healing and growth can be realized.*

Group Meditation Steps

SET YOUR IDEAL (Service, Love, Wisdom, Peace, Harmony, etc.)

PREPARE AND CLEANSE:

POSTURE- Spine straight, feet on floor (or crossed at ankles), close hands by joining thumb and index finger.

HEAD AND NECK EXERCISES-

- Eyes closed throughout exercise!
- Slowly drop head to chest 3x
- Slowly drop head back 3x (like looking up at the sky)
- Rotate head slowly to look over your right shoulder 3x
- Rotate head slowly to look over your left shoulder 3x
- Drop head to chest and rotate it clockwise to your right shoulder, to the back of your head, and to your left shoulder. Return to position of your chest and to an upright position 3x
- Do the above in a counter-clockwise movement 3x

BREATHING EXERCISES-

Close off left nostril with your finger (of either hand), breathe in through your right nostril a slow deep breath and exhale through your mouth while consciously saying for each count in your mind:

- Love
- Peace
- Truth

Close off your right nostril with your finger (of either hand), breathe in through your left nostril, and exhale through your right while consciously saying for each count in your mind:

- Harmony
- Wisdom
- Joy

CHANT – Take in a deep breath and bring forth the OM chant (Aaa-Reee-Ooo-Mmmmm) aloud for 8-10 seconds (3x).

PRAYER OF PROTECTION – "As I open myself up to the unseen forces, I surround myself with a holy robe of pure white light" (envision pulsating white light outlining your body).

AFFIRMATIONS – "As I seek to know myself, I ask the universe to help me blot out all fear and doubt, and fill my life with love and peace" (Spoken aloud 3x) "Peace…Be Still" (Spoken aloud 1x) . **Then SILENCE for 5 minutes.**

HEALING FOR OTHERS / PLANET – "I send white healing light to (name individuals to yourself) and the planet.

✐ Group Participant Evaluation Form

Participant _____ Date _____

How did you hear about the therapy group?

_____ Counselor _____ Referral _____ Friend _____ Other (please specify)

Was the group leader effective in explaining the dynamics of sexual assault for each session so that you could understand it?

_____ Yes _____ No _____ Not Sure

Was the group curriculum itself clear and concise?

_____ Yes _____ No _____ Not Sure

What session(s) of the group curriculum did you find most helpful? Check all that apply:

_____ Session 1-Breaking the Silence, Our Stories, Who We Are

_____ Session 2- Dealing with PTSD or Why Am I Not Myself?

_____ Session 3- Understanding It Wasn't Your Fault

_____ Session 4- How the Assault Changed Your Life

_____ Session 5- Survival Skills & Coping Mechanisms

_____ Session 6- Challenging Negative Schemas

_____ Session 7- Anger – The Backbone of Healing

_____ Session 8- Your Support System & Personal Safety Plan

_____ Session 9- Healing Sexually

_____ Session 10- Building Self Esteem

_____ Session 11- Mourning Your Losses and Moving On

_____ Session 12-The Pursuit of Happiness & Group Termination

What session(s) did you find the least helpful? List numbers from above list.

Session(s)# _____ All were helpful _____

Were the group exercises helpful?

_____ Yes _____ No _____ Not Sure

Which session(s) would you like to spend more time on?

Session(s)# _____ No preference _____

What aspect of the group program would you change?

_____ Day _____ Time _____ Session Topic _____ Group Leader _____ Other

_____ I like it the way it is.

Have you experienced any change in behavior since coming to group?

_____ Yes _____ No _____ Not Sure

Has your thinking about yourself and your relationships changed as a result of coming to group?

_____ Yes _____ No _____ Not Sure

What Life tools are you now aware of that could be helpful to you in the future? Check all that apply:

_____ Personal Insight _____ Emotional Safety Planning _____ Boundary Settings

_____ Other (specify)

Do you feel empowered after participating in the group?

_____ Yes _____ No _____ Not Sure

Would you recommend group to other survivors of sexual assault?

_____ Yes _____ No _____ Not Sure

We invite you to offer any comments that you feel will be helpful to us:

_____

_____

_____

_____

_____

_____

_____

_____

_____

_____

THANK YOU FOR PARTICIPATING IN GROUP!

✒ GROUP TERMINATION INSPIRATION

You can search throughout the entire universe for someone who is more deserving of your love and affection than you are yourself, and that person is not to be found anywhere.

You yourself, as much as anybody in the entire universe deserve your love and affection.

The Buddha

✒ THE THREE "M'S TO LIVE BY

MEDITATION:
Contemplating your life, becoming self-aware, finding inner peace

MODERATION:
Reducing all unhealthy obsessive habits and patterns of behavior

MOTIVATION:
Establishing goals and plans to retain a sense of hope in your life

BIBLIOGRAPHY AND REFERENCES

Adams, Carol, and Jennifer Faye. (1989).*Free of the Shadows: Recovering from Sexual Violence.* Oakland, CA: New Harbinger Publications.

Altman, Donald. (2011). *One Minute Mindfulness: 50 Simple Ways to Find Peace, Clarity, and New Possibilities in a Stressed Out World.* Novato, CA: New World Library.

Anderson, Janet (2008). *Sexual Assault and Substance Abuse.* Research & Advocacy Digest, The Washington Coalition of Sexual Assault Programs.

Association for Specialists in Group Work. (2004). *Special issue on Teaching Group Work.* Journal for Specialists in Group Work. Volume 29, Number 1.

Atkinson, Matt. (2012). *Resurrection After Rape: A Guide to Transforming from Victim to Survivor.* Oklahoma City, OK: RAR Publishing.

Beck, Aaron. Cognitive distortions. Retrieved from: http://education-portal.com/academy/lesson/aaron-beck-cognitive-therapy-theory-lesson-quiz.html#lesson.

Beck, Judith S. (1995). *Cognitive Therapy: Basics and Beyond.* New York: Guildford Press.

Belmont, Judith A. (2006). *TIPS: 86 Treatment Ideas and Practical Strategies for the Therapeutic Toolbox.* Eau Claire, WI: Premier Publishing and Media.

Bourne, Edmund J. (2005). *Anxiety and Phobia Workbook.* 4th Ed. Oakland, CA:New Harbinger Publications.

Brossman, Sandra C. (2001). *Awakening to Oneness: A Personal Guide to Wholeness and Inner Peace.* Aurora, OH: Greenleaf Book Group LLC.

Buddha. Retrieved from www.brainyquote.com/quotes/authors/b/buddha.

Burgess, AW; Holmstrom, LL (1974) Rape Trauma Syndrome. American Journal of Psychiatry, 131 (9): 981-98470).6 (www.ncbi.nlm.nih.gov/pubmed/441.

Centers for Disease Control and Prevention, (2009). Adverse Childhood Experiences Study. (http://www.cdc.gov/ace.)

Chu, James A. and Elizabeth S. Bowman. (2002). Trauma and Sexuality: The Effects of Childhood Sexual, Physical, and Emotional Abuse on Sexual Identity and Behavior. New York: Haworth Medical Press Inc.

Cohen, J.A. & Mannarino, A.P. (2008). Trauma-focused cognitive behavioral therapy for children and parents. Child & Adolescent Mental Health, 13(4), 158-162.

Copeland, Mary Ellen.(2001). *The Depression Workbook*. 2nd Ed. Oakland, CA: New Harbinger Publications.

Corey, Marianne S. and Corey, Gerald. (2006). *Groups: Process and Practice*, seventh edition. Belmont, CA: Thomson, Brooks/Cole publishers.

Courtois, Christine. (1988). *Healing the Incest Wound*. New York: W.W. Norton & Co.

Courtois, Christine. (1999*). Recollections of Sexual Assault: Treatment Principles and Guidelines*. New York: W.W. Norton & Co.

Davis, Laura and Ellen Bass. (1988). *The Courage to Heal: A Guide for Women Survivors of Childhood Sexual Assault*. 3rd Ed. New York: Harper Collins Publishers.

Davis, Laura. (1990).*The Courage to Heal Workbook: For Women and Men Survivors of Childhood Sexual Assault*. New York: Harper Collins Publishers.

Dolan, Yvonne. (1991*). Resolving Sexual Abuse: Solution-Focused Therapy and Eriksonian Hypnosis for Adult Survivors*. New York: W.W. Norton & Co.

Grayson, Carla E. (2005). Substance Abuse/Women As Victims. Journal of Traumatic Stress, 18(2) 137-145.

Gregory, Barry M. (2010). *Cognitive Behavioral Therapy Skills Workbook: Practical Exercises and Worksheets to Promote Change*. Eau Claire, WI: Premiere Educational Solutions.

Hall, Kathryn. (2004) *Reclaiming Your Sexual Self: How You Can Bring Desire Back Into Your Life*. Hoboken, NJ: John Wiley & Sons, Inc.

Hay, Louise L. (2004). *You Can Heal Your Life*. New York: Hay House, Inc.

Health Consequences of Sexual Abuse (1993). The Harvard Mental Health Letter, 9 (7).

Herman, Judith L. and Lisa Hirschmar. (1981). *Father-Daughter Incest*. Cambridge, MA: Harvard University Press.

Hunter, Bronwyn A. (2012). Characteristics of sexual assault and disclosure among women in substance abuse recovery homes.. Journal of Interpersonal Violence, p18.

Kessler, R.C. (2000). Posttraumatic Stress Disorder: The Burden to the Individual and to Society. Journal of Clinical Psychiatry, 61(5) 4-12.

Kilpatrick, Dean G. (2000). The Mental Health Impact of Rape. The National Violence Against Women Prevention Research Center, Medical University of South Carolina. Retrieved 2013 from http://www.musc.edu/vawprevention/research/mentalimpact.shtml.

Kilpatrick, D.G., et al. (2003). Violence and Risk of PTSD, Major Depression, Substance Abuse/ Dependence, and Comorbidity: Results from the National Survey of Adolescents. Journal of Consulting and Clinical Psychiatry, 71(4), 692-700.

King, M., Coxell, A & Mezey, G. (2002) Sexual Molestation of Males: Associations with Psychological Disturbance. British Journal of Psychiatry, 181:153-157.

Kool, R.. and Lawver, T. (2010). Play therapy: Considerations and applications for the practitioner. Psychiatry (Edgemont), 7(10), 19-24. Retrieved January 2013 from http://www.ncbi.nlm.nih.gov/pmc/articles/PMC2989834/.

Levey, Joel and Michelle Levey. (1998). *Living in Balance: A Dynamic Approach for Creating Harmony and Wholeness in a Chaotic World.* New York: Fine Communications MJF Books.

Lisak, David. (1994). The Psychological Impact of Sexual Abuse: Content Analysis of Interviews With Male Survivors. Journal of Traumatic Stress, 7(4):525-548.

Male Sexual Victimization Myths and Facts, retrieved August 2009 from www.malesurvivor.org. Adapted from a presentation at the 5th International Conference on Incest and Related Problems, Biel, Switzerland, August 14, 1991.

Maltz, Wendy. (2012). *The Sexual Healing Journey: A Guide for Survivors of Sexual Abuse,* 3rd Ed. New York: Harper Collins Publishers.

Matsakis, Aphrodite. (1996*). I Can't Get Over It: A Handbook for Trauma Survivors.* 2nd Ed. Oakland, CA: New Harbinger Publications.

Matsakis, Aphrodite. (1998). *Trust After Trauma: A Guide to Relationships for Survivors and Those Who Love Them.* Oakland, CA: New Harbinger Publications.

McKay, Matthew, M. Davis and Patrick Fanning.(1997). *Thoughts and Feelings: Taking Control of Your Moods and Your Life.* Oakland, CA: New Harbinger Publications.

Miller, Alice. (2009). *Breaking Down the Walls of Silence: The Liberating Experience of Facing Painful Truth.* New York: Perseus Books Group.

Myss, Caroline. (1996*). Anatomy of the Spirit: The 7 Stages of Power and Healing.* New York: Three Rivers Press.

Petracek, Laura J. (2004). *The Anger Workbook for Women.* Oakland, CA: New Harbinger Publications.

Postmus, Judy L., Editor. (2013). *Sexual Violence and Abuse: An Encyclopedia of Prevention, Impacts, and Recovery.* Santa Barbara, CA: ABC-CLIO, LLC.

Raja, Sheela. (2011) Adopting Universal Trauma Precautions: Serving patients who have survived sexual violence. College of Medicine and Dentistry, University of Illinois.

Resick, Patricia A. (1996). *Cognitive Processing Therapy for Rape Victims: A Treatment Manual.* Newberry Park, CA: Sage Publications.

Rogne, Carol.(2012). *Self Esteem: Respecting and Valuing Ourselves.* Denver, CO: Outskirts Press.

Russell, Diane, E.H. (1986). *The Secret Trauma: Incest in the Lives of Girls and Women.* New York: Perseus Books Group.

Saleebey, Dennis. (2012). *The Strengths Perspective in Social Work Practice.* Boston, MA:Allyn/ Bacon & Longman, p. 129.

Schiraldi, Glenn R.(2000). *The Post Traumatic Stress Disorder Sourcebook: A Guide to Healing, Recovery, and Growth.* Los Angeles, CA: Lowell House.

Schiraldi, Glenn R. (2001). *The Self Esteem Workbook.* Oakland, CA: New Harbinger Publications.

Severe PTSD Damages Children's Brains, (2007). Science Daily, Stanford University Medical Center.

Shapiro, Robin. (2010). *The Trauma Treatment Handbook: Protocols Across the Spectrum.* New York: W.W. Norton & Co.

Silverman, Jay G. et al. (2001) Dating Violence Against Adolescent Girls and Associated Substance Use, Unhealthy Weight Control, Sexual Risk Behavior, Pregnancy & Suicidality. Journal of the American Medical Association, 285(5): 572.

Thomas, R. Valorie and Pender, Debra A. (2007). Association for Specialists in Group Work:

Best Practice Guidelines 2007 Revisions. Retrieved June 2014 from http://www.asgw.org/pdf/ Best_Practices.pdf.

Toseland, Ronald W. and Robert F. Rivas.(2005*). Introduction to Group Work Practice.* 5th Ed. Boston, MA: Pearson Education Inc. by Allyn & Bacon.

Ullman, Sarah E. (1998). Does Offender Violence Escalate When Rape Victims Fight Back? Journal of Interpersonal Violence, 13 (2): 179-192.

US Department of Justice, 2012, National Crime Victimization Study 2008-2012. Retrieved from http://rainn.org/get-information/statistics/frequency-of-sexual-assault.

US Department of Justice. (2005). National Crime Victimization Study. Retrieved from http:// rainn.org.

US Department of Justice Office on Violence Against Women (2010), National Criminal Justice Reference Service reports, Myths and Facts about Sexual Violence.

Van der Kolk, Bessel A. et al. (2005). Disorders of Extreme Stress: The Empirical Foundation of a Complex Adaptation to Trauma. Retrieved November 2012 from http:///www.traumacenter. org/products/pdf_files/SpecialIssueComplexTraumaOct2006JTS3.pdf

Vermilyea, Elizabeth G. (2000). *Growing Beyond Survival: A Self-Help Toolkit for Managing Traumatic Stress.* Baltimore, MD: Sidran Press.

Warshaw, Robin. (1994). *I Never Called It Rape: The Ms. Report on Recognizing, Fighting and Surviving Date & Acquaintance Rape.* New York: Harper Perennial:66.

Woititz, Janet G. (1989). *Healing Your Sexual Self.* Deerfield Beach, FL: Geringer Health Communications Inc.

Wood, Wendy A. (1993). *Triumph Over Darkness: Understanding and Healing the Trauma of Childhood Sexual Abuse.* 2nd Ed. Hillsboro, OR: Beyond Words Publishing Inc.

Yalom, Irvin D. (1995). *The Theory and Practice of Group Psychotherapy*, 4th Ed. New York: Perseus Books Group.

Yalom, Irvin D. and Leszcz, Molyn. (2005). The Theory and Practice of Group Psychotherapy, 5th Edition. New York: Basic Books, p.272.

Zierler, S. et al (1991). Adult Survivors of Childhood Sexual Abuse and Subsequent Risk of HIV Infection. American Journal of Public Health, 81(5).

Zur, O. (2011). Taking Care of the Caretaker: How to Avoid Psychotherapists' Burnout. Online Publication by Zur Institute. Retrieved 2/16/14 from http://zurinstitute.com/burnout.html..

Printed in the United States
By Bookmasters